REVENGE OF THE GRANNIES

by

James Russell

COMEDY SCREENPLAY

Purchasing this script does not authorize performance rights. Please contact publisher before performing to negotiate terms & conditions. This script may or may not be available for production.

To locate publisher, in the event we move type: "James Russell Publishing" in any Internet search engine. Try also an updated edition of the Thomas Register at your library.

DEDICATION TO:
"It is a good thing to give thanks unto the Lord." Psalm 92.1

A THOUGHT TO PONDER:
There are over 800 promises in the Bible. Have you read them?

TITLE PAGE

"Revenge of the Grannies"

© Paul-760-704, October 28, 1997 by James Russell.
ISBN # 0-916367-25-8 (Print Version)
ISBN # 0-916367-44-4 (e-book Version)

James Russell Publishing
780 Diogenes Drive
Reno, NV 89512
Web: www.powernet.net/~scrnplay
E-mail: scrnplay@powernet.net
SAN # 295-852X

"Revenge of the Grannies"

Written by James Russell
First prepress Printed © April 1999.
First Printed edition © September 2000 0-916367-25-8.
E-book edition August © 2000 ISBN 0-916367-44-4
Printed in the USA

THIS BOOK CAN BE PURCHASED FROM

-- Amazon.Com Books - www.amazon.com
-- Barnes & Noble - www.barnesandnoble.com or bookstore in your area.
-- Borders Books - www.borders.com or bookstore in your area.
-- Books A Million - www.booksamillion.com or bookstore in your area.
-- Chapters (Canada) - www.chapters.ca or bookstore in your area.
-- Lou's Books, 5647 Atlantic Ave, Long Beach, CA 90805 (213)423-1403.
-- Opamp Technical Books, 1033 N. Sycamore Ave, Los Angeles, CA 90038 (800)468-4322.
-- Varsity Books - see Internet or college bookstore.
-- Walden Books
-- Your local bookstore and e-book outlet kiosks.
-- We have a bookstore listing on our Web site.

Any bookstore can order this book. Just give them this number: ISBN # 0-916367-25-8 and our SAN #295-852X.   To locate us in the event we move type: James Russell Publishing in any Internet search engine.

* * * * * * *

800 PROMISES

The Lord has declared over 800 promises in the Bible. Have you read them?

* * * * * * *

FADE IN:

INT. MD-80 JET AIRCRAFT - NIGHT   PRESENT

MARGARET (68) curly white hair, glasses. Surrounded by rowdy
BIKERS. She's knits a hat. Peers out window to see,

CRIMINALS loot stores, drag people from cars. Fires rage
light up hell itself.

BIG DADDY (35) leader of Sad Devils motorcycle gang wears
W.W.II German helmet, studded leathers, scraggly Santa Clause
beard. With heavily tattooed arm slaps MAD DOG (30) on ear.

                    BIG DADDY
          Mad Dog, lookie here. I bet'cha
          granny like to ride ya Jap hog.

Bikers giggle as children. Margaret nails Big Daddy a cold
stare. MAD DOG'S pimpled face invokes shivers.

                    MAD DOG
          Hey grandma? Promise I'll have ya
          home by nine.

More giggles. Mad Dog's smile reveals one upper tooth.
Margaret smirks, knits with determination. Her fists
clenched tightly on needles.

Fasten seat belt annunciator PINGS!

                    CAPTAIN (V.O.)
          Hi, folks. Descending to Lost
          Angus International. Say a little
          prayer for me.

                    BIKERS
              (randomly)
          "Get off my seat belt, jerk."
          "Hey, that's my belt." "Ah, shut
          up." "Let go, I'll call the cops."

Margaret drops ball of yarn into isle.

                    CAPTAIN (V.O.)
          Thank you for flying Pelican
          Airlines. Three crash landings
          this year, but I survived!

Bikers chins drop, warily eyeball each other.

Jet pitches nose-first BANG. Wings scrape runway, silver
sparks and smoke spray by windows. Squeal of grinding metal.

Margaret calmly knits as Bikers scream like teenage girls on
a roller coaster. They pray MOS with rosary beads.

Jet stops. Bikers charge exit door, trip in tangled yarn.
Margaret rises from seat, but panicky bikers place their hand
on her head push her back down as they pass her by.

After three attempts she sits. Anger flashes in her eyes as
white knuckles crack her cane. Cabin vacated.

Margaret gathers belongings, approaches exit. CAPTAIN steps
from cockpit, smiles. He's dressed like a biker. She
screams.

INT. AIRPORT - NIGHT

MARGARET hustles to gate 21. Her cane twists like a crowbar
to separate a couple hand-in-hand.

BIKERS shove people out of their path. BIG DADDY attempts to
steal a lollipop from baby carriage. BABY GIRL cries.

                    MAD DOG
          Ha! I'll show'ya how, Big Daddy.

Mad Dog reaches for balloon floating above another carriage.
Yellow liquid squirts on Mad Dog's hand. BABY BOY in biker
clothes laughs.

EXT. TAXI STAGING AREA - NIGHT

MARGARET raps side window of limousine with cane.

                    MARGARET
          Young man, these windows and door
          panels bulletproof?

                    LIMOUSINE DRIVER
          Mama, that's two inch bank teller
          glass. Stops bullets, meteorites,
          flying hubcaps, horny six-hundred
          pound grandpas. Step in, babe.

Margaret slips into back seat. BIKERS pass by, hold
briefcases, escorted by Lost Angus POLICE.

SERIES OF SHOTS / VARIOUS LOCATIONS - NIGHT

- - Leave airport, MARGARET enters uncivilized territory.
Beer cans, rocks, hubcaps strike limousine. Pizza pie smears
windshield.

- - Gangs of youths loot stores, fist fights, trash cans
burn, random gunfire.

- - MARGARET crouches low, eyes level to window sill. DRUG
DEALERS approach limousine at stop light, offer to sell
drugs, handguns, brassieres.

- - MARGARET enters the peaceful City of Heavenly Hills.
Arrive at a mansion laced with barbed wire. MARGARET enters
the house, steps to,

INT. LIVING ROOM - NIGHT

MARGARET flips on TV. NARRATOR v.o. details street gangs
taking over West Hollywierd. News clips reveal POLICE retreat
from a gang riot. Margaret punches eleven numbers on Mickey
Mouse phone.

                    MARGARET
                (on phone, angry)
            I am ready.

Margaret hangs up, clicks out TV, strolls to bed.

INT. DINING ROOM - DAY

Sunrise filters through barbed wire windows. MARGARET sits at
dining table. Snoopy phone rings.

MAID (18) sets breakfast. She's dressed in satin blue gown.
LOGO on apron reads, "Starving Teenagers Maid Service For
Those Who Can Pay Our Price."

Margaret fumbles to answer phone.

                    MARGARET
                (on phone)
            This is America! I'm not gonna
            take it anymore!

Unintelligible v.o. from receiver.

                    MARGARET
                (continuing)
            What do you mean I'm too old?

FLUFFY a hairless cat (Cornish Rex) leaps to lap.

                    MARGARET
                (continuing)
            You just get me the stuff. I'll
            take care of the rest.

Margaret slams phone, grumbles to herself about being too old.

Daughter, JENNIFER (38) enters, brushes her long golden hair,
gazes into jewel-studded mirror. She wears a lavish pink
evening gown fit for a Queen's inauguration. Ruby red
slippers.

                    JENNIFER
            Now where on earth are you going?

                         MARGARET
                 Broken Feather Indian bingo. I
                 promised the girls I would be on
                 the team. It's only a two month
                 tournament.

Jennifer grabs Margaret's pocketbook, they struggle. Fluffy
hisses, leaps to floor. Margaret yanks pocketbook back.
Jennifer's mirror crashes to floor. Fluffy growls, dashes out
of room. Margaret exits to,

INT. DEN - DAY

MARGARET paces floor, cigarette in hand. JENNIFER enters,
hand on hip. FLUFFY claws expensive rug.

                         JENNIFER
                 You know I can't sleep when you're
                 carousing with that bingo crowd.
                 I wish you would make new friends.
                 And you should quit smoking too.

Margaret exhales an outrageous billowing cloud of smoke.

                         MARGARET
                 I might as well die happy!

Fluffy sneezes, gags, runs along small red carpet, leads to
a lavish English castle cat house. Margaret aims a shaking
finger at Jennifer, then, points to Fluffy who peeks out of
castle.

                         MARGARET
                         (continuing)
                 Stop giving him whipped cream. It
                 gives him gas and he stinks up the
                 place.

Jennifer cradles, kisses Fluffy's nose. She smells gas, puts
Fluffy down. Margaret chews on a prune.

                         JENNIFER
                 Stop blaming the cat! You should
                 switch to apples.

Jennifer models in mirror, swipes hips with hand.

                         JENNIFER
                         (continuing)
                 Men don't seem to conceive I have
                 bowel problems.

                         MARGARET
                 Keep fooling around and I
                 guarantee you'll wish you had
                 constipation.

                    JENNIFER
          Oh, mother. I swear, your whole
          world revolves around intestinal
          contractions and illegitimate
          children. The men I know respect
          me.

Margaret grabs purse, exits front door to,

EXT. DRIVEWAY - DAY

MARGARET steps into her Silver Shadow Rolls Royce, powers
down window. JENNIFER stands by front door.

                    JENNIFER
          Why can't you find a decent
          husband? Settle down and be a
          good granny?

Margaret burns rubber as she drives away.

INT. CAR / HOLLYWOOD BLVD. - DAY

MARGARET blasts horn as she passes cars. Pulls in to,
"Thelma's Gun's." THUGS window-shop, wolf-whistle at
Margaret.

EXT. SIDEWALK - DAY

MARGARET ignores THUGS and enters, Thelma's.

EXT. SENIOR CITIZEN HALL - DAY

Large billboard reads, "Welcome to heavenly hills senior
center. Friday night bingo pro championships! Free beer,
hot dogs, dietary fiber cocktails! $5 cover charge. No old
men admitted. Be there or be square!"

SKINHEAD (70) wears black studded leather jacket, green
Mohawk haircut, razor-blades dangle from ears. He parks
MARGARET'S car. She keeps her distance, holds folded white
cardstock and purse.

INT. SENIOR CITIZEN HALL - DAY

MARGARET enters dim-lighted hall. A smoke-filled night club
atmosphere. Piercing heavy-metal MUSIC on jukebox. GRANNIES
play bingo on candlelit tables, video arcade and pinball
machines.

Margaret yanks cord to jukebox, hall falls silent. Grannies
murmur. She steps to stage, removes handgun from purse,
fires into floor POW! Everyone freezes.

INT. BASEMENT BOILER ROOM - DAY

Janitor SAMUEL GOBLINGAB (50), skinny, nervous demeanor,
shifty eyes. He turns a valve, jumps as bullet splits steel
pipe. Hissing steam fills room, alarm buzzes.

                    SAMUEL
          I think I screwed up.

He races upstairs. Boiler ALARM fades as Samuel approaches
first floor.

INT. HALLWAY BY MAIN HALL - DAY

SAMUEL hears a BANG from main hall. Cautiously tiptoes to
the door, index fingers pinched. Sign on door, "Old Men Keep
Out." He peeks into keyhole.

                    MARGARET
          Look at yourselves. Spending your
          children's inheritance while the
          city falls into the hands of drug
          dealing deviants.

CROWD so still you could hear a pin drop. A GRANNY burps,
all heads turn toward her with scolding eyes.

                    MARGARET
                 (continuing)
          You saw the evening news. A
          street hoodlum pushed an elderly
          woman down. As she lay helpless he
          kicked her saying, "Give me your
          money you miserable bag of
          misery." We need to take a stand!

Crowd expresses agreement with soft "Yeah's." "Right on
sister."

                    FIRST SPECTATOR
          We need more cops. Picket City
          Hall.

                    MARGARET
          Forget the cops! The courts give
          criminals so many rights the only
          thing the Man can arrest is stray
          dogs monsooning hydrants.
                 (beat)
          No, we need to do more than that.
          An eye for an ear, a tooth for a
          bone.

Margaret unfolds white cardboard sign, "Join MEBOM, Mothers
End Brutality of Mankind!" Crowd cheers with a mighty roar,
canes rap tables and floors.

                         MARGARET
                     (continuing)
                 Society cares less about us. We
                 are nothing but a feckless
                 commodity to be disposed of. We
                 have rights. We demand respect.
                 We shall be honored.

Hall falls deathly silent. SARAH (68) stands, she has a
snarling BULLDOG on leash.

                         SARAH
                 I want to kick some buns.

                         MARGARET
                 Join with me to take back Lost
                 Angus.

Crowd fails to respond. She thinks quickly.

                         MARGARET
                     (continuing)
                 They plan to take away your Social
                 Security!

Crowd erupts in riotous anger. GRANNY stands, angrily waves
cane in air, others duck her swings.

                         SECOND SPECTATOR
                 I'll break their backs and pluck
                 their teeth if they touch my
                 Social Security. I mean it!

Crowd stirs, expressions of hostility.

                         MARGARET
                 We'll take back our streets with
                 granny power. Let's show those
                 criminals what medicine mothers of
                 all mothers can prescribe.

Margaret waves pistol in air. Crowd cheers. Another
spectator stands. She's 90 years old.

                         THIRD SPECTATOR
                 Give me a machete. I have nothing
                 to lose. I want to be a mebom!

Crowd ecstatically slaps fists and canes on tables chant,
"Mebom! Mebom!" Margaret waves pistol in air POW!

Bullet ricochets. Grannies duck. Bullet exits through entry
door near keyhole. Crowd comes to order.

INT. HALLWAY / BY DOOR - DAY

Bullet parts SAMUEL'S hair. He runs down stairs.

BACK TO SCENE

> MARGARET
> Deep within us all resides a
> little Rambo, a gallant Dirty
> Harry and a powerful Terminator.
>
> (beat)
> Close your eyes. Call their
> spirits.

Hall still and quiet

> GRANNIES
> (random whispers)
> "Come Rambo, I know you are
> there." "Dirty Harry, it's time to
> awaken." "Moe, Larry, Curly rise
> and shine it's time to play."
> "Terminator, come forth!"

INT. BOILER ROOM - DAY

Boiler explodes.

BACK TO SCENE

Bolt of lightening flashes, climbs walls. Chandeliers sway,
building shakes and creaks. Buzzing electrical arcs sizzle
along their clothes.

Miraculously, instilled with courage and vigor, each feel
their arm muscles bulge.

Margaret selects four leaders. CORINNE, BERTHA, DEBBIE, and
PENELOPE. They step on stage. SARAH hops on.

> SARAH
> I was married to a private
> investigator. I can help.

> MARGARET
> Welcome.

They all shake hands.

INT. BOILER ROOM - DAY

SAMUEL dashes into steamy boiler room. Rips telephone off
wall, stabs three digit number.

                           SAMUEL
                        (on phone)
                Hello? We gotta bunch of wild
                grannies planning to attack Lost
                Angus! Come to the Heavenly
                Senior Citizens Center. Pronto.

EXT. SENIOR CENTER / FRONT DOORWAY - DAY

SAMUEL, confused, stands by door as grannies rush out back
door. In b.g. MARGARET nods. SARAH approaches Samuel, points
cane to his nose. BULLDOG growls.

                           SARAH
                Don't you rat on us, Samuel
                Goblingab. I'll tan your rump with
                battery acid.

Sarah dashes out back door just as COPS arrive. With a
running jump she clears a four-foot tall picket fence and
disappears with Bulldog.

Sirens blare o.s. Samuel turns, Margaret slips out back door
undetected.

Cops charge building in a drug raid manner. SERGEANT
approaches Samuel.

                           SAMUEL
                The old prunes were here a minute
                ago, but now they're all gone.

                           SERGEANT
                That's okay, we came for the
                donuts.

Sergeant waves his arm.

                           SERGEANT
                        (continuing)
                Okay boys, move in and take 'em!

With battle cries, cops rush tables, stuff donuts in paper
bags, fill thermos bottles with beer and wine.

                           SERGEANT
                        (continuing)
                Hurry up guys before they come
                back.

EXT. FRONT STEPS - DAY

COPS rush from building, they ignore Samuel.

                         SAMUEL
               Wait, I'm tellin' ya grannies
               formed a militia called, "Mebom"
               to take over Lost Angus.

                         COPS
                    (randomly)
               "Coffee's cold, man." "Hey, you
               took more than your share of
               donuts." "Hurry up!" "I want the
               beer."

Cops race out, enter cruisers.

                         SAMUEL
               I'll get you for this. You guys
               didn't leave me any donuts.

Chocolate jelly donut slams into Samuel's face SPLAT!
Another whacks groin OW! Ten more splatter him.

INT. MARGARET'S MANSION - DAY

MARGARET sits on couch, browses military catalog. Eyes
locked on a mini-submarine.

Doorbell rings, four leaders enter, BERTHA, DEBBIE, PENELOPE
and CORINNE. CORINNE (65) slim build, short curly white hair.

                         CORINNE
               We alone?

                         MARGARET
               Yes. Jennifer took Fluffy to the
               dentist. I wish she would stop
               feeding him sweets.

She hands Margaret "Guns R Us" catalog, then pretends to
grasp a pistol with both hands.

                         CORINNE
               We bought a ton of this stuff.
               The next relative insults me. Pow!

PENELOPE (50) salt/pepper hair, wears glasses. Baffled look
on her face. She steps to Margaret, points to radio-
controlled airplane on magazine back cover.

                         PENELOPE
               Perfect for reconnaissance.

DEBBIE (72) short curly silver dyed hair, wears glasses. She
grabs the catalog. Flips a few pages, returns it to
Margaret.

                              DEBBIE
                    Look at page forty-seven.

Magazine page - photo of six handsome men dressed in various
combat uniforms.

                              DEBBIE
                                (continuing)
                    Aren't they gorgeous?

                              MARGARET
                    Did you buy any?

                              DEBBIE
                    What do you think I am a call girl?

Margaret slips Debbie a scornful eye.

                              MARGARET
                    Debbie, I'm talking about the
                    uniforms not the men. Get serious!

                              PENELOPE
                    What's a call girl?

BERTHA (80) dark brown hair, gentle voice.

                              BERTHA
                    A call girl is a lady that never
                    hangs up on obscene callers. Like
                    Debbie, they don't know what no
                    means.

                              DEBBIE
                    Well at least I know what a man
                    wants!

                              CORINNE
                    That reminds me of the soap opera,
                    As The Earth Ages. Frank told
                    Sally what he really wanted was
                    understanding. It was so
                    romantic. A perfect gentleman.

                              DEBBIE
                    Get a life Corinne. Frank wants
                    sex and he'll lie to get it.

Corinne's visibly upset.

                              CORINNE
                    Frank is not that type of man.

>   DEBBIE
>   Yeah right. Like when he told his
>   last girlfriend sex is the only
>   cure for his hemorrhoids.

Corinne fidgets.

>   CORINNE
>   It cured him didn't it?

Debbie points a scolding finger.

>   DEBBIE
>   He never had any hemorrhoids!

>   CORINNE
>   He did too!

>   DEBBIE
>   He did not!

Margaret throws magazine to floor.

>   MARGARET
>   (snappy)
>   Cut it out both of you.

Margaret, frustrated, rises from couch, enters,

INT. KITCHEN - DAY

MARGARET pours "Fantasic Stools" fiber mix into glass of
orange juice. Corinne and Debbie argue o.s. PENELOPE enters.

>   PENELOPE
>   I suppose there is no turning back?

>   MARGARET
>   The stakes are high, Penelope. We
>   lost, Lost Angus.

>   PENELOPE
>   What's our chances?

Margaret reveals a vacant expression. They enter,

INT. LIVING ROOM - DAY

CORINNE and DEBBIE sulk. Arms folded, chins buried deep into
chests. Room strangely quiet.

>   MARGARET
>   Okay, Frank's an honest liar. Now
>   stop pouting and listen-up.

Margaret removes manila envelopes from briefcase labeled,
"Top Secret." Hands them out.

                    MARGARET
                 (continuing)
            These plans will self-destruct in
            seventy-two hours. I'll see you
            at the base tomorrow night.

Margaret opens front door, girls leave.

EXT. DRIVEWAY - DAY

Each drives an expensive car. JENNIFER pulls into driveway
in her pink Ferrari. As DEBBIE drives away CORINNE screams
out her window.

                    CORINNE
            Frank is not a liar!

Jennifer's baffled. Steps out of car, FLUFFY in arms,
approaches MARGARET.

                    JENNIFER
            Now what did you do?

INT. LIVING ROOM - DAY

JENNIFER and MARGARET enter living room. Margaret stares into
framed PHOTO of a drunken stubble-bearded old man on
fireplace mantle. A real hoboe.

                    MARGARET
            He was a good man, Jennifer. He
            never hurt anybody. Always did
            whatever he could to help people.
            He was gunned down like a dog, for
            what? A measly empty wallet and a
            bottle of beer.

With photo in hand, Margaret turns to Jennifer.

                    JENNIFER
            Fluffy only had two cavities.

Margaret peers into Fluffy's mouth, sees more gold than
teeth. Fluffy hisses at photo, swipes paw at it, leaps away.

Margaret replaces photo on mantle, gazes passionately at the
drunken man.

                         MARGARET
              He always said I was too passive.
              That if the world is to change
              everyone must take a stand. Do
              the right thing. Evil blooms when
              few cut the weeds.

Margaret turns, faces Jennifer.

                         MARGARET
                    (continuing)
              Jennifer, do you remember when he
              took us to the beer festival?

                         JENNIFER
              I remember. Stop feeling guilty,
              it's not your fault. Crime is
              random, affects anyone at anytime.
              Nobody could have prevented what
              happened. It just happened that's
              all. We can't change the world.

                         MARGARET
              No, not that! The time he fell
              off the bar stool landing on a
              Doberman. That's criminal! Dogs
              shouldn't be allowed to have teeth.

INT. MAYOR'S OFFICE / 10TH FLOOR - DAY

SAMUEL crouched low in a tiny chair across from Mayor JIM
GOODMAN (45). Samuel's chin barely reaches desktop. Violin
case near Samuel's feet.

Police Chief, DON SNITCH (50) stands by Goodman.

                         SAMUEL
              I'm telling you the truth. I seen
              it with my own eye.

                         SNITCH
              What did your other eye see?

                         SAMUEL
              Half of what my other eye seen.
              I don't see too good out of it.

Goodman sits up, leans over desk, a psychiatrist smile.
Fiddles with his rattlesnake head bola tie with extended
fangs.

                         GOODMAN
              Now Samuel. Why would a bunch of
              little old ladies want to take
              over my city?

                    SAMUEL
          They don't feel safe.

Goodman angrily rises from chair. Palms press so hard on the
desk, the wood cracks.

                    GOODMAN
          You saying I can't run my city?

Samuel stutters, raises hands in air.

                    SAMUEL
          I didn't say that. The grannies
          said it.

                    SNITCH
          I have no fear of grannies. Okay
          Samuel, what's your angle? What
          do you really want?

Snitch scratches his rear with index finger.

                    SAMUEL
          I can go undercover for you and
          expose the grannies.

                    GOODMAN
          Then what?

                    SAMUEL
          If I succeed, I figure you could
          get me a promotion.

                    SNITCH
          What kind of promotion?

Snitch picks teeth with same finger.

                    SAMUEL
          Chief latrine inspector.

Goodman squats in chair, feet on desk, lights a cigar with a
naked woman lighter, twists cigar in his teeth.

                    SNITCH
          He's asking too much. Throw the
          bum out.

Snitch grabs Samuel by the arm.

                    GOODMAN
          We can work something out here.

                    SNITCH
          You don't believe this chimney
          sweep, do you?

                         GOODMAN
               I do.

Samuel gloats to Snitch, defiantly extends tongue. Snitch
raises backhand to slap Samuel.

Samuel opens violin case, places toilet plunger inches from
Snitch's nose. Dried dark matter on plunger.

                         SAMUEL
               One more step. You'll regret it.

Snitch gazes cross-eyed into rubber suction cup. His mouth
droops, beads of sweat roll on his face.

Goodman places cigar in his mouth, slowly rises from chair
with an open-hand gesture of friendship.

                         GOODMAN
               Now boys, boys. Let's not get
               carried away.

                         SAMUEL
               You tell him to keep his hands off
               me or I'll plunge him!

Goodman places hands on both of their shoulders, gently
massages.

                         GOODMAN
               Samuel, why can't we be friends?
               Put the knife down. Let's talk
               business.

Goodman's cigar blows clouds of smoke. Samuel's eyes well
with tears, sneezes up a horrendous mucous, swallows it as a
snake swallows a huge pig. Snitch gags.

                         GOODMAN
                    (continuing)
               Sam, Don Snitch is a good friend
               of mine and the best Police Chief
               Lost Angus ever had. Now you
               don't want to hurt my friends do
               you?

Samuel puckers, pouts, wags head. Goodman pulls a hanky,
wipes Samuel's tears. Samuel grabs hanky. Goodman snatches
plunger, tosses to trash. Snitch moves quickly behind
Goodman's desk for protection.

                         GOODMAN
                    (continuing)
               Both of you relax. Sit down,
               Samuel. I'd like to make you a
               proposal.

Samuel stands, upset.

                    SAMUEL
          I'm not a homosexual, sir.

Snitch's finger vibrates, aims to Samuel.

                    SNITCH
          Is there something wrong with that?

                    GOODMAN
          Sit down!

Samuel sits. Goodman offers Samuel a cellophane wrapped
cigar. Samuel places to lips, lights it with cellophane in
place.

Goodman and Snitch exchange a look, then they sit.

                    GOODMAN
                  (continuing)
          I take care of my friends.

Samuel sits up attentively. His nose rests on desk, fingers
by his nose. He looks like a puppy dog begging for food.

                    SNITCH
          Who's the leader of this granny
          gang?

                    SAMUEL
          She has wrinkles, older than old,
          like a, grandmother.

Snitch's eyes roll up.

                    SNITCH
          What's her name?

                    SAMUEL
                  (to Snitch)
          I don't like talking to you.
                  (to Goodman)
          Do I have to talk to him?

Goodman nods. Snitch withdraws.

                    SAMUEL
                  (continuing; to
                  Goodman)
          I don't know the woman. But I'll
          find out. It's a deal?

                              GOODMAN
                    You keep tabs on these grannies.
                    Tell me what they do, where they
                    are. I want every name, detail,
                    time, place, event, with photos.

Samuel lands Snitch a snub conceited nod.

                              GOODMAN
                         (continuing)
                    You get me the inside scoop and
                    I'll make you the most honored
                    Chief Latrine Inspector Lost Angus
                    ever had.

Samuel stands, leans over desk. He's full of joy. His face
turns serious.

                              SAMUEL
                    And, I get the Movie Star commodes
                    in Hollyweird, too?

                              GOODMAN
                    It can be arranged.

Samuel blows a smoke ring, transforms to shape of a toilet
bowl. It gently floats to Snitch.

Snitch blows hard, watches it dissipate into random vapor.

Snitch opens door with butler cordiality, extends palm for
Samuel to exit. Samuel turns to Goodman, frantically shakes
his hand.

                              SAMUEL
                    You won't be sorry, sir. I've
                    read many James Bond books.

                              GOODMAN
                    I'm sure you have.

Samuel steps out, lands a defiant look to Snitch.

INT. RECEPTION AREA - DAY

SAMUEL passes the SECRETARY (30).

SNITCH approaches Samuel with toilet plunger. Samuel takes
it, removes pieces of dark matter, eats it.

Secretary gags. Snitch and GOODMAN grossed out. Samuel looks
to Snitch, grins.

                              SAMUEL
                    Chocolate chips.

Samuel enters hallway, exits to elevator.

                    SNITCH
          You believe that dimwit nincompoop?

                    GOODMAN
          My wife said she saw a rowdy horde
          of grandmothers playing football
          at Roosevelt High School. They won!

Goodman nervously paces floor, cracks knuckles.

                    GOODMAN
                  (continuing)
          It's getting crazy around here.
          We can't take any chances.

                    SNITCH
          C'mon Mayor, you can't be afraid
          of a few aerobic grannies that
          hang out in bingo parlors.

Secretary enters, holds rag to mouth.

                    SECRETARY
          Excuse me. I need to go home. My
          grandmother is in trouble.

                    GOODMAN
          What kind of trouble?

                    SECRETARY
          She sprained her hand trying to
          break a brick. She's studying to
          be a Kaolin Monk. May I leave?

Goodman lands Snitch a concerned expression.

                    GOODMAN
          Of course you may. Who's
          substituting?

                    SECRETARY
          Mrs. Crabapple.

MRS. CRABAPPLE enters the room. She's a granny.

Goodman's face turns white.

INT. PENELOPE'S HOME / DEN - DAY

PENELOPE shows CORINNE her dinosaur dung collection. Appear
as rocks, though shaped as doggie doo doo.

Penelope grunts, lifts a bowling ball size coiled fossil.
Corinne marvels.

                         PENELOPE
                It's a T-Rex pooper. I found it
                at LaBrea tar pits. It's worth a
                hundred-forty grand.

                         CORINNE
                I'll tell you what. I'll offer
                you two of my most prized
                portfolio manager trading cards.

Corinne pulls a stack of cards, resembles baseball cards,
displays PHOTOGRAPHS of notable investors. Fans cards as a
pro magician would along her arm.

Penelope snatches two cards in a blink of the eye.

                         PENELOPE
                Ooh, La La! You got Sam Bucks and
                Lester Investor. Okay, it's a
                deal, but I also want Bob Moola,
                or no deal.

Corinne shakes hands, hands Penelope the third trading card.
Places dung in her pocketbook on floor.

When she picks it up, pocketbook handles tear away. Fossil
rolls on her foot OUCH!

EXT. DESERT BASE / MOJAVE DESERT - NIGHT

C-130 aircraft loading door open, brightly lit. Forklift
busily unloads crates onto trucks. Trucks and jeeps pass by.

MARGARET, CORINNE, DEBBIE, PENELOPE, BERTHA enter a portal to
underground bunker.

INT. BUNKER - NIGHT

Beehive of activity. GRANNIES in military uniform unpack
weapons. Straight-faced granny MP's stand at strategic
points.

A door labeled, "Command and Control."

INT. COMMAND AND CONTROL - NIGHT

MARGARET, CORINNE, DEBBIE, BERTHA, PENELOPE stand by
electronic wall map of Southern California. Margaret's laser
pointer highlights Lost Angus City Hall.

Margaret wears blue uniform as Commander in Chief. Bertha in
Navy Petty Officer white. Others in desert fatigues.

On the map, a moving image. GOODMAN speaks to crowd on front
steps of City Hall. Margaret places laser on Goodman.

                         MARGARET
          The Honorable Mayor, Jim Goodman
          is not so honorable. He is the
          mastermind. We need to capture him
          and bankrupt his crime business.
          But it won't be easy.

Margaret moves laser to SNITCH who sits behind Goodman. He
nibbles a hamburger.

                         MARGARET
                       (continuing)
          He's under the Mayor's thumb.
          This guy is, Wimpy, reincarnated.

Laser passes by a MAN'S head in the crowd.

                         DEBBIE
          Stop! Focus on that thing.

Screen zooms-in, focuses on back side of subject's head.
LASER selects, "Menu, Front View." The man's face turns
forward.

                         DEBBIE
                       (continuing)
          That's our janitor, Samuel
          Goblingab!

                         BERTHA
          Who's that in the lower left
          corner?

Laser squiggles in Margaret's shaky hand on a BLACK MAN (30)
dressed in black-studded leathers. Mean looking guy.

                         MARGARET (V.O.)
          Spike, leader of the L.A. Cowboy's
          motorcycle gang. Rivals of the
          Sad Devils. Momentarily they have
          a truce.

Margaret moves laser to MEXICAN MAN (20) who wears a white
ten-gallon hat.

                         MARGARET (V.O.)
                       (continuing)
          He's the shot caller of the East
          L.A. street gangs. They call him
          Spiny.

Margaret flicks laser to the "Quit" menu, screen fades. Small
lines slowly draw on screen. A picture of Uncle Sam pointing
a finger. The uncle is a granny.

Top caption, "I Need You!" Bottom caption, "Proud to be a
MEBOM." Margaret hands each a pill.

                    CORINNE
          My goodness, cyanide? Just like
          in the spy movies.

                    MARGARET
          Not cyanide. It's a stool
          softener. Can't perform if you're
          constipated. Down the hatch girls.

They stand in a circle, place pill between lips, reach for
cocktail glass of water. They toast.

                    MARGARET
                 (continuing)
          Grannies rule!

INT. / EXT. MARGARET'S HOME - NEXT DAY, MORNING

MARGARET in civilian clothes, just finished breakfast. MAID
removes plates from table.

A knock at the door. Margaret opens door, it's a delivery
MAN (25).

Semitractor trailer attached to flatbed in driveway in b.g.
On flatbed - large shipping container with multinational
inscription. One in English reads, "Norwegian Iron Works
Ltd."

Delivery man excited, hands Margaret Bill of Lading.

                    DELIVERY MAN
          I've never made a delivery to
          Heavenly Hills before.

          I normally handle the industrial
          route. Nice home. Are you rich?

Margaret smiles.

                    DELIVERY MAN
                 (continuing)
          What's in that container?

                    MARGARET
          Why do you ask?

                    DELIVERY MAN
          Curious. I've hauled equipment in
          my day, but this is the most
          turbulent load I've ever had.

Margaret radiates a sheepish look, signs Bill of Lading,
hands it back.

                    DELIVERY MAN
                  (continuing)
            I never heard such a racket.
            Every time I stopped I heard
            strange eerie howls.

Margaret's eyes squint, in deep thought.

                    MARGARET
            It's a whale.

                    DELIVERY MAN
            A what?

                    MARGARET
            You know, a big fish. Movie
            studio's shooting another dinosaur
            flick. This time, it's a flesh
            eating whale in Lake Tahoe.

                    DELIVERY MAN
            Why would they ship it to Heavenly
            Hills?

                    MARGARET
            Young man, do you have a
            grandmother?

Delivery man removes hat, scratches ear.

                    MARGARET
                  (continuing)
            You ask your grandmother why they
            shipped a big reptile to a little
            old granny like me. Her guess is
            as good as mine.

Margaret writes a street address.

                    MARGARET
                  (continuing)
            Here, take this and deliver it to
            Bones Shipyard in Long Beach.
            That's where it should be.

Delivery man apologizes, jumps in truck, leaves. Margaret
bolts to couch, retrieves purse, exits house, starts car,
races to,

EXT. BONES SHIPYARD - DAY

- - Small dilapidated industrial building. White SEAGULL
pilfers trash can by front door. Finds a paper bag, tosses it
to ground, violently rips bag with beak. A small piece of a
cheeseburger tumbles out.

- - Gull swallows it, stares right at us HAW! HAW! HAW!

INSERT translation - "Where's the fries?"

Gull violently rips into bag again. French fries tumble out.

- - Another GULL arrives and eats them. First gull tries to
steal back his meal, but is rebuffed by the raiding gull,
loses feathers in the struggle.

MARGARET, in civilian clothes, impatiently knocks on door.
Shutter slides open, two eyeballs appear. Door creaks opens,
rust flakes from hinges. It's CORINNE. Margaret enters.

              MARGARET
        Hurry up. Close the door.

              CORINNE
        What are you so uptight about? Got
        the runs or something?

              MARGARET
        Close the door, now!

Corinne slams the door.

              CORINNE
        Gee whiz you don't have to be such
        a grouch.

              MARGARET
        Something is wrong.

Margaret walks to a small office. Corinne follows.

INT. OFFICE - DAY

BERTHA sits at desk, reads a "True Divorce" magazine. She
hears footsteps, jams magazine in drawer as MARGARET and
CORINNE enter. PENELOPE on couch, snores. All in civilian
clothes.

              BERTHA
        Why do you both look so solemn?
        Did Frank break up with Elizabeth?

              CORINNE
        He was, but his nurse convinced
        him not to.

Truck horn o.s. HONK!

              MARGARET
        Remain silent no matter how
        strange things may appear.

Margaret and Corinne jog to garage door, press red button.
Door opens, clacks loudly.

Margaret guides the truck backing container into garage. She
shouts "Stop" just before the cab enters.

DRIVER kills engine, exits, greets Margaret.

              DELIVERY MAN
        Didn't I just see you in Heavenly
        Hills?

              MARGARET
        How was the trip?

Faint metallic thuds emit from container. Margaret's worried
eyes momentarily shift to container.

              DELIVERY MAN
        That's what I was telling you
        about. And it howls too.

A howl accompanies the amplified clanging noise.

              MARGARET
        At my age I can't even hear cat
        calls anymore.

              DELIVERY MAN
        You sure that's a whale?

              MARGARET
        Would a grandmother lie?

Corinne clenches a fist.

              DELIVERY MAN
        No way! My grandmother never lied
        to me, ever.

He's nervous.

              DELIVERY MAN
                (continuing)
        Frank is going to Disneyland. I
        sure don't want to miss that
        episode. I better hit the road.
        My wife gets furious when her
        supper isn't cooked.

Driver fast-steps to rig, starts engine. Black clouds of
swirling smoke enter garage from exhaust stacks.

Margaret brushes smoke from her face. Driver guns engine,
flatbed jerks forward, container slides, slams to floor
KABOOM!

MOMENTS LATER

Diesel smoke cleared, garage door closes. Bertha exits
office, cautiously approach container. Muffled hollow groans
from container. Soft thuds.

                    BERTHA
          Oh my goodness. What on earth is
          that noise?

                    CORINNE
          Sounds like a buffalo!

Corinne snags a crowbar, places it under latch lever. Bertha
helps Corinne pry. Plastic seal snaps, lever lets go with a
POP! Crowbar flies, rings on concrete floor.

Margaret nervously approaches container, hesitates, slowly
swings open container door. Corinne and Bertha stand silent
with big eyes of anticipation. Corinne steps behind Bertha.

A beautiful neon pink object comes into view. A black tag
dangles from it. Margaret removes tag. In reverse type it
reads, "To Remove Contents Pull Lever Once And Stand Clear."
Howling and banging increases.

Margaret grabs lever, the "thing" slowly slides out onto
garage floor, smooth as silk, a soft rolling sound. It's a
pink World War II class mini-submarine.

                    BERTHA
          It's beautiful!

Sub has gold plated hand railings, chrome periscope. A jet
black General Electric chain-fed Gatling gun on forward deck.

Duel launch missile forks mounted on forward superstructure
painted metalflake blue.

Ladder from deck to floor permanently attached to side. The
girls touch its surface with gleeful excitement. BLAM! They
jump back in a flash of fear KABOOM! CLANG! CLANG!

                    CORINNE
          Merciful heavens, the torpedoes
          are loose!

Margaret climbs ladder, sees hatch padlocked. Motions for
bolt cutters. Bertha hands them to her. She snaps the lock,
then steps back. Nothing happens.

Hand wheel on hatch turns. Hatch barely open. Margaret holds
bolt cutters over shoulder as a baseball bat. Motions with
hand shaped as a pistol for Corinne to get a gun.

Submarine hatch - two eyeballs cautiously shift left to
right, mechanical-like. Hatch opens more. Soot-covered
skinny face emerges.

It's an OLD MAN (90). Margaret kicks hatch open. Old man
looks up to her.

                    MARGARET
          Come out of there real slow-like.

Frail old man shakes from fear and his age, slowly rises on
deck. Corinne has him covered with a Colt 45.

                    MARGARET
                 (continuing)
          Reach for the sky. Now!

He tries to raise arms, but only raises them halfway.

                    OLD MAN
                 (Norwegian accent)
          I can't. I got bursitis rigor
          mortis.

Senses the old man can't harm her, Margaret lowers bolt
cutters to her side.

                    MARGARET
          Who are you? What are you doing
          here?

Old man hesitates, his head gently quivers as if attached to
a spring.

                    OLD MAN
          I work for Oslow Ordinance. A
          subcontractor who supplies
          torpedoes, missiles and guns to
          defense contractors.

                    MARGARET
          How did you get here?

                    OLD MAN
          I was setting torpedo fuses when
          suddenly the hatch closed. I fear
          it was no accident. My boss
          thinks I'm dating his wife.

Margaret's astonished. Bertha's eyes wide with delight.

                    MARGARET
          You date at your age?

                    OLD MAN
          Oh sure, but my bosses wife is
          ninety-seven. Too old for me, but
          he still thinks something's going
          on.

                    MARGARET
          What's your name?

                    OLD MAN
          Olsen.

                    MARGARET
          Olsen what?

                    OLD MAN
          Just Olsen. I can't remember my
          last name.

                    MARGARET
          Mr. Olsen, you are now a prisoner
          of war. Off the deck. Keep your
          hands where I can see them.

They slowly descend ladder. Corinne grasps pistol mimicking
Dirty Harry. Bertha has compassion in her eyes, approaches
Olsen, eyeballs his skinny build with affection.

                    BERTHA
          My goodness gracious he's starving.
                    (to Olsen)
          You hungry?

                    OLSEN
          I could go for a sea lion
          sandwich, but McDonald's would be
          okay.

They walk to the office. Margaret enters first.

INT. OFFICE - DAY

MARGARET sits, places feet on desktop, thinks fast. PENELOPE
still snores on couch.

                    MARGARET
          I have a proposition for you Mr.
          Olsen

                    OLSEN
          I'm not that kind of man, Miss --

                    MARGARET
         That's not what I had in mind.

OLSEN appears rejected.

                    MARGARET
              (continuing)
         I can get you back home again.
         Would you like that Mr. Olsen?

                    OLSEN
         Very much, Madame.

                    MARGARET
         How versed are you in running this
         submarine?

Olsen tries to stand to attention as best he can. He salutes,
clicks his heels.

                    OLSEN
         I served in both world wars with
         honors, sir. Navy, sir.

Margaret senses his change of behavior. She stands up,
military posture.

                    MARGARET
              (playing him)
         You're in the Navy, Olsen. As
         Commander of Special Forces I
         promote you to Chief Engineer.
         Congratulations.

Olsen salutes. Margaret returns salute.

                    OLSEN
         Thank you, sir!

                    MARGARET
         We use code names in the Navy for
         our Chief's. Your name is Lanky.
         Do you understand me?

                    LANKY
         That's my last name. How'd you
         know?

                    MARGARET
         What did you say?

LANKY straightens up, clicks heels, salutes.

                    LANKY
         I said, aye aye, sir!

                         MARGARET
                      (to Bertha)
             I want this boat fitted for active
             duty and on station tonight. I'll
             send the crew at twenty-one-
             hundred hours. Be ready!

BERTHA and Lanky salute. Margaret turns to walk away, stops
for a moment, faces Lanky.

                         MARGARET
                      (continuing)
             You need a bath, mister.

Bertha has a mischievously happy look on her face. Margaret
and Corinne walk to the exit.

                         BERTHA (V.O.)
             Come Lanky, I'll help you get into
             the tub.

INT. BIKER BAR - NIGHT

The two rival motorcycle gangs coexist inside TUGBOAT ANNIE'S
biker bar. Loud rock MUSIC on jukebox. They shoot pool,
scratch lottery tickets, clean shotguns, throw daggers at
dart board.

BIG DADDY, shirtless, sits on a fat GIRL's lap. She POPS
pimples on his back with pointed edge of a gold plated, ivory
skull-handled Bowie knife.

SPIKE, leader of the L.A. Cowboys gang, sits at bar, warily
eyeballs Big Daddy.

Spike slams his drink down, slowly approaches Big Daddy's
table. Expression on face cold as ice. MUSIC stops.
Absolute silence.

Big Daddy slowly leans over, eyes intently fixed on Spike,
reaches for leather jacket on floor. Spike's boot stomps his
hand, pins it to wood. Big Daddy looks up at Spike towering
over him.

                         SPIKE
             It's time to get it on.

Big Daddy pushes the heavy boot from his hand. Spike steps
back. Big Daddy rises, raises index finger as if saying,
"One moment please." Puts leather jacket on.

Girl hands him the Bowie knife. He slams it down into the
table, pierces Joker on deck of cards. Big Daddy's hand
grasps knife handle.

Spike's open-stretched hand approaches. Big Daddy grabs hold
of Spikes wrist. They dance cheek-to-cheek. A slow dance with
arms fully extended. Soft MUSIC plays. They dance under a
chandelier.

                    BIG DADDY
               (whispers in ear)
          We need to stop meeting like this.

                    SPIKE
          Listen motorhead, Goodman's
          expecting his cut. You got to
          deliver the money, tomorrow,
          twelve noon.

Spike's earring tickles Big Daddy's nose. Big Daddy tries to
blow it away. Spike's eyes widen.

                    BIG DADDY
          Where?

                    SPIKE
          Pier thirteen. The Mayor's new
          boat. You can't miss it. Yacht's
          name is, Honesty.

                    BIG DADDY
          Why do I have to make the delivery?

                    SPIKE
          It's the will of the Mayor.

                    BIG DADDY
               (heated)
          Yeah, and what are you doing?

Big Daddy pushes Spike away forcefully. His eyes hard,
buries finger into Spike's chest.

                    BIG DADDY
               (continuing)
          Don't step on my toes.

                    SPIKE
          Oh, alright then. Cease your
          sniveling. I'll do it.

Spike's gang snivels, shake heads, pout.

CLOSING TIME

Bikers leave. A lone granny KAREN BLINTZ (65) busily cleans
up the place. She stands on a chair, removes a "bug" from
chandelier. Places it in bra.

EXT. BONES SHIPYARD - NIGHT

SAMUEL spies on shipyard. FIVE GRANNIES in white Navy
uniform tug a rope, submarine slips a ramp.

They climb aboard, stand on deck as they drift onto a dark
sea. Samuel, excited, fumbles for camera to get a shot, but
he's too late.

EXT. PHONE BOOTH - MORNING

SAMUEL on telephone.

                    SAMUEL
          I swear, Mr. Goodman. I seen it
          with my own eye --

Dial tone. Samuel bites lower lip. A BOY sells Girl Scout
cookies. Sam pays him three dollars, takes the box, walks
away.

                    BOY
          Call the cops, I've been robbed!

GIRL SCOUT pulls a gun, robs Samuel of the cookies. COP pulls
up. Girl scout points to Samuel, he runs away. Cop pursues.

INT. MEXICAN RESTAURANT / EAST LA - DAY

SPINY sits in a booth, acts like a Mafia boss. Latino GANG
MEMBERS everywhere. His Lieutenants sit with him. Rap MUSIC
sets mood.

                    SPINY
          That's not good enough! East L.A.
          is my turf. Nobody cuts into our
          action. They better back off or
          it's gonna be war.

                    LIEUTENANT
          Homes. Ya gotta think and be
          real. That's the Mafia!

                    SPINY
          Tell ya somethin' homeboy. There's
          more of us than them. East side's
          outta bounds. Gimme the phone.

Spiny jabs dial buttons.

WAITRESS delivers two crispy beef tacos. We don't see her
face, but she's got a great body.

Spiny eats taco with one hand, speaks in phone, sauce drips
on receiver.

                          SPINY
                   (continuing; smooth)
               Hey Hombre, how's business?

                       GOODMAN (V.O.)
               Spiny, I told you not to call me
               at the office.

                          SPINY
               Don't be hostile, my man.

                       GOODMAN (V.O.)
               What do you want?

                          SPINY
               The Italians losing table manners.
               They make a mess of my
               establishment. I don't want them
               in my barrio.

                       GOODMAN (V.O.)
               I'll give them a pizza --

                          SPINY
               Pizza? Tacos here, homes.

                         GOODMAN
               They want a pizza the action. Get
               it?

Spiny's enlightened.

                         GOODMAN
                      (continuing)
               I'll satisfy their hunger.

                          SPINY
               Hey my man, ya got heart.
               Excelente! Fantastico! I got pesos
               Senor. Six big ones. Sunday,
               seven p.m. Santa Monica vista.

                       GOODMAN (V.O.)
               Great.

Spiny hangs up. Waitress delivers a round of Margarita's. As
she turns, she's a Latino granny. LOLITA GONZALES (65). She
grins.

EXT. DESERT BASE - DAY

MARGARET, CORINNE, DEBBIE, PENELOPE escort two GRANNIES
dressed in civilian clothes whom we never saw before.

Corinne, Debbie and Penelope dressed in desert fatigues, wear
helmets with red letters, "MEBOM".

Arm patches - Fist holding blue lightning bolt reads, "Granny Power."

SERIES OF SHOTS

- - GRANNIES in military garb speed-draw Colt 45 revolvers, shatter whisky bottles on a wood fence.

- - ENTOURAGE walks to next area where GRANNIES practice judo. Two M1A1 Abrams TANKS pass close by.

- - MARGARET points to sky as GRANNIES parachute from a tower. GRANNY SOLDIER (90) drags her chute mentions it's a "Piece of cake" gallops off to jump again.

- - In b.g. two tanks fire at each other. Flour filled bags explode on contact PLOOF!

- - GRANNIES crawl under barbed wire, machine gun fires live ammo overhead. GRANNY behind the gun wears a baseball hat with the words, "Stand Up!"

- - A cheating GRANNY by-passes barbed wire obstacle course. She hides, sits under a Joshua tree.

- - Group of NEW RECRUITS jog with a loudmouth granny DRILL INSTRUCTOR with a deep hoarse voice. The new recruits repeat each sentence after the DI.

>   DRILL INSTRUCTOR
>   Get your bones on the road. Keep
>   in step you big old toad. Your
>   mamma told you you're too old. She
>   was wrong you knocked her cold.

>   DRILL INSTRUCTOR
>   (continuing)
>   Atten, hut!

GRANNIES fall in line, gasp for air. Ready to graduate GRANNIES run by them at remarkable speed. The new recruits stare at them with amazement.

>   DRILL INSTRUCTOR
>   (continuing)
>   Don't you look at them. You're
>   not worthy to look at them.

Paces the line.

>   DRILL INSTRUCTOR
>   (continuing)
>   When I'm finished with you bag of
>   worms you'll be doing the same,
>   but faster.

Nose-to-nose with a recruit.

>   DRILL INSTRUCTOR
>   (continuing)
>   You think I'm hard on you? Just
>   wait till you hit the streets of
>   L.A.

Steps back, points to barracks.

>   DRILL INSTRUCTOR
>   (continuing)
>   Now get your sorry asses out of my
>   sight.

Drill Instructor angrily stomps out of view. MARGARET slowly
approaches group of new recruits.

>   MARGARET
>   You must be strong if you wish to
>   live.

In b.g. a GRANNY leaps from parachute tower. Her chute fails
to open. She hollers HELP!

Splats the ground just beyond a small rise. Cloud of white
flour rises into air.

Another GRANNY does the same thing, then another. Three
grannies straggle over the rise, covered in dusty flour.

Drill instructor disgusted, hands on hips.

>   DRILL INSTRUCTOR
>   You bunch of morons, you're
>   supposed to pull the little white
>   string. The little white string!

>   PENELOPE
>   (to Margaret)
>   I don't feel I can kill anyone.
>   Even if they deserve it.

>   CORINNE
>   I agree. This thing is going too
>   far.

>   MARGARET
>   Who said were gonna kill anybody?

>   PENELOPE
>   What? With all these combat
>   troops and ammo and were not going
>   to kill things?

Armored Personnel Carrier (APC) rear ramp drops. Grannies with M1 rifles rush out, scream like Marines hitting a beach.

Margaret stops a SOLDIER. She wears thick eye glasses. They exchange salutes.

> MARGARET
> At ease, Private. Ammo clip.

> SOLDIER
> Yes, sir.

Soldier reaches into her belt removes a black clip. Margaret inspects brass cases and gray caps. Everything appears in order.

> MARGARET
> (to soldier)
> Have you ever shot anyone before?

> SOLDIER
> (stuttering)
> I haven't, sir.

> MARGARET
> Lock and load, soldier.

Soldier inserts clip into M-1 SNAP!

> MARGARET
> (continuing)
> You see the grunt sitting under
> that tree?

Soldier removes eye glasses, squints. After some difficulty she nods, puts glasses back on.

> MARGARET
> (continuing)
> Shoot her! Do it! That's an order.

Penelope, Corinne, and Debbie horrified, stupefied, can't speak, jaws locked open.

Soldier takes aim, empties magazine on full auto TAT! TAT! TAT!

Bark from the tree rips to shreds. Dust kicks up all around the GRUNT. Grunt runs, bullets beat a path into her legs and up her back.

She spins, falls face-down, lies silent in a haze of dust.

Soldiers rush to her aid. She looks dead. Arms sway limply as they carry her into the portal entrance.

>   DEBBIE
>   (to Margaret)
>   Are you crazy? You killed her!

>   MARGARET
>   Your out of line, soldier!

Margaret walks briskly to portal. Entourage follows. As
they pass the dead soldier surrounded by MEDICS they stop to
observe.

Margaret looks briefly at the grunt, but doesn't stop. She
appears heartless. She enters Command and Control room.

Grunt arouses, appears in great shape as she sits up. She's
a little sore as she rubs her leg.

>   GRUNT
>   Hot dog, that was a blast. I
>   wanna do it again.

Everyone amazed. Margaret exits command room.

>   MARGARET
>   That's what rubber bullets do.
>   They have enough punch to put you
>   down, but leave no permanent
>   injuries.
>   (beat)
>   But that's not the case with the
>   enemy. They have tangible bullets
>   and real death to deliver. So you
>   need to be on your toes.
>   (beat)
>   Now get out there. Train hard.
>   We don't have much time. Get
>   cracking!

Two grannies in civilian clothes enter a black limousine,
slip on dark sunglasses.

>   FIRST GRANNY
>   (to Margaret, coldly)
>   A little sloppy.

>   SECOND GRANNY
>   It's your reputation, your future
>   at stake, not ours.

They leave. License plate, "MEBOM." Margaret bites lip.

INT. SUBMARINE / LONG BEACH HARBOR - DAY

The GRANNIES and LANKY conduct sea trials. They screw up
royally. Sub arches up out of the water reenters nose-first
like a dolphin.

EXT. BEACH - DAY

The sand boils. SAMUEL's head pokes up. He raises
binoculars to his eyes. Only his hands and head protrude.
He scans the harbor.

BACK TO SCENE

Sub surfaces, bow straight up, breaks the surface, rises ten-
feet then slips below the surface like a fish taking an
insect.

INT. SUBMARINE - DAY

LANKY shouts instructions. Pure panic. BERTHA repeats his
instructions with authority. She enjoys herself.

CREW dumbfounded, randomly pull levers, press buttons.
Exactly what the Three Stooges would do. Sub tilts and
rolls. You'd be dizzy if you were inside.

EXT. BEACH - DAY

SAMUEL looks through binoculars, intently surveys the bay.
A lone white SEAGULL lands, blocks Samuel's view.

Gull slowly waddles to the lens. Samuel's hand waves to shoo
bird away.

                    SAMUEL (V.O.)
              Get out of here!

Gull flies away, then returns eye-to-eye with Samuel. The
typical angry gull stare.

                    SAMUEL (V.O.)
                    (continuing)
              Darn you. Go away.

A hand flips a spray of sand at the gull.

WIDER VIEW

Gull flies away, returns more determined than ever. Gull
lands twenty-feet from Samuel.

Samuel drops binoculars, waves hand, makes hissing sounds,
then peers into binoculars.

Gull doesn't budge an inch. Its head turns left and right
examining the situation. Takes a few steps closer and stops.

Makes five quick quack calls like a duck. Samuel ignores it,
looks in binoculars.

Gull approaches, comes around to the back of Samuel's head. Samuel's eyes search for the gull. Gull inches from Samuel's ear HAW! HAW! HAW!

Sam's face contorts in pain. His swinging arms can't reach gull. Gull's beak rips a chunk of hair from Samuel's scalp. OUCH!

Gull swallows, gags, spits it out. Out comes another chunk of hair RIP! Then another. Gull tears hair out at a feverish pace. Samuel hollers, "Help!"

YOUNG COUPLE deeply in love stroll along beach oblivious to Samuel's cries. Gull sees them approach, makes a quick exit.

Four bare feet inches from the back of Samuel's head. They trip over him, sand sprays in Samuel's face. Gull returns. Pecks Samuel's head like a woodpecker.

In desperation, Samuel flings binoculars in air, misses gull, binoculars crash on his head THUD! He squints in pain, but it frightened the gull away.

Gull flaps its wings, gains altitude, circles menacingly like a buzzard.

A small white object falls. It grows larger as it descends. Splats on Samuel's forehead.

Gull looks right at us, smiles, soars victoriously into the horizon.

INT. SUBMARINE / CONTROL ROOM - DAY

CREW gains control of the submerged submarine. LANKY'S exhausted, elbows on desk, leans over slightly, fingers gently rub temples.

A wine glass, half-full of pink liquid and a bottle labeled, "Babushka's Peptic Fire Extinguisher" on desk.

BERTHA peers into periscope with arms draped over spindles. Crew members stare into portable TV.

ON TV

TWO GRANNY'S argue in a laundromat over whom will do Frank's laundry. His briefs in a Tug-Of-War tear in half.

INT. SUBMARINE / TORPEDO ROOM - DAY

Frederick's of Hollywood clothes draped on pipes and valves. Huge bra fitted to nose of two torpedoes. Three GRANNIES read magazines.

A few article headlines, "How to pick up men at bingo games."
"Nine ways to lie to your doctor and never get caught." "How
to make money following teenagers." "Diamonds are forever,
but make him take you to Vegas too!" "Shooting craps, secrets
of a pro." "Get incredibly rich with baby-sitting business."

INT. SUBMARINE / CONTROL ROOM - DAY

BERTHA peeks into periscope, snaps fingers to LANKY, sees a
YACHT moored to a dock.

Motorcycles ride dock, approach yacht. It's Big Daddy's
gang, the SAD DEVILS.

                    BERTHA (V.O.)
              Something's going down. That's
              Mayor Goodman's yacht!

Bikers board yacht, hand money to COP on deck. WOMAN in a
pink bikini lounges on deck.

Bertha lifts microphone. A computer monitor screen reads,
"Encryption activated. Dialing Command & Control. Line
busy. Please try again. Thank you for using G.U.P.-Cellular.
Special discounts after 5 p.m."

Bertha snaps off computer, presses red button on wall.
Battle station alarm activates AHROOGAH! Annunciator light
flashes, "Alert."

INT. USS LIONFISH - DAY

U.S. Navy nuclear attack submarine LIONFISH patrols
submerged. SONAR OPERATOR places hand on headphone. Face
strains as he listens intensely.

He flips switch on sonar scope. A small arrow tracks a
dashed line to the source of the noise. He calls out to
CAPTAIN JASPER FUNGITIS (32).

                    SONAR OPERATOR
              Captain, I'm picking up a
              European submarine alarm signal.
              Originating inside Short Beach
              harbor.

                    CAPTAIN FUNGITIS
              Confirm anomalies.

                    SONAR OPERATOR
              No errors, sir.

                         CAPTAIN FUNGITIS
                    There must be. No attack
                    submarine can navigate this pithy
                    harbor without getting rammed.
                    A new secret weapon? Call the
                    Admiral!

EXT. SEA LEVEL / ABOVE LIONFISH - DAY

INFLATABLE BUOY rises to surface. Antenna rises.

                         OPERATOR (V.O.)
                    Pentagon, department of defense.
                    May I help you?

                         CAPTAIN FUNGITIS (V.O.)
                    Admiral Kapoochi please.

                         OPERATOR (V.O.)
                    Please hold.

BACK TO SCENE

MUSIC from Lionfish PA system o.s. Then static and squeals.
RADIO OPERATOR flips switches to isolate problem with no
results. Whacks console with rubber mallet CLUNK! Static
gone. MUSIC resumes.

SPLIT SCREEN / INT. PENTAGON / INT. PIZZA PARLOR - DAY

ADMIRAL KAPOOCHI (50) and RESTAURANT EMPLOYEE (18) argue on
telephone. Admiral speaks on red phone. Admiral's ugly,
pimples, big ears, overweight slob. Restaurant employee has
a face you'd love to slap.

                         ADMIRAL KAPOOCHI
                    How many times must I tell you I
                    don't like cheese on my pizza?

                         RESTAURANT EMPLOYEE
                    Admiral Kapoochi the grouch. Am
                    I correct?

Kapoochi angrily unzips and zips his fly.

                         ADMIRAL KAPOOCHI
                    Listen kelp head. If you want
                    Pentagon business you shape up or
                    ship out!

                         RESTAURANT EMPLOYEE
                    Don't you threaten me you sailing
                    bag of tail wind. I'll tell my
                    uncle Jungulitis your attitude
                    needs calibrating.

Kapoochi screams as fly pinches his underwear.

                    ADMIRAL KAPOOCHI
          You mean Secretary of Defense,
          Antonio Nicola Morocco Julius
          Jungulitis?

                    RESTAURANT EMPLOYEE
          You better be nice to me!

BACK TO SCENE

FUNGITIS clicks off intercom, gawks to crew in disgust.

                    CAPTAIN FUNGITIS
          He's ordering pizza on the
          emergency communications line
          again. We need to take matters
          into our own hands. Battle
          stations!

INT. SUBMARINE - DAY

GRANNIES each at their assigned posts. Two push a torpedo
into launch tube. Words on torpedo, "With All My Love,
Grandma."

They close the door, screw firing pin assembly into tube
door, attach electrical wire to pin.

They stand ready. LANKY steps to BERTHA as she peers into
periscope. She sees COP on yacht place stacks of money on
deck.

Cop and BIKERS step onto pier. The WOMAN still sunbathes on
deck.

                    BERTHA
          Fire one!

- - CREW MEMBER punches red fire button with her bony finger.
Torpedo exits tube SWOOSH!

- - BERTHA'S POV - Torpedo fishtails a stream of bubbles
straight to yacht.

- - WHAM! Yacht and pier break up inside a boiling orange
and black fireball. BIKERS and their bikes flip into the
air. Seagulls take to the air.

- - BIKERS in water hold on to debris. BIKER floats on top
of the WOMAN. He sees air bubbles leak air from her bikini.
Biker panics, squeezes woman's breasts to stop air leaks.

                    BIKER
                 (to woman)
          Hold your breath!

She's an inflatable doll.

INT. SUBMARINE - DAY

GRANNIES cheer, leap wildly. LANKY and BERTHA slap hands.

INT. LIONFISH - DAY

SONAR OPERATOR painfully rips earphones off. A blast of
noise emits.

EXT. BEACH - DAY

SAMUEL lounges on a blue umbrella covered beach chair,
playfully plunges sand with toilet plunger.

Yacht explodes. Samuel leaps to his feet, grabs camera,
snaps pictures. He wears a knife on his belt.

BIKER on inflatable doll floats in the waves shouts HELP!
Samuel dives into the surf.

INT. LIONFISH - DAY

A computer monitor reads, "Chemical ordnance pressure wave
detected. Notify captain."

Captain FUNGITIS stands by monitor.

                    CAPTAIN FUNGITIS
                    (euphoric)
          It's about time we get to shoot
          something. This is it men, the
          real thing. Man battle stations.
          Phase red!

A red light flashes, but no audible alarm.

                    CAPTAIN FUNGITIS
                    (continuing)
          Stay at 400 feet. One ping.

Sonar operator sends a PING!

                    SONAR OPERATOR
          Reflection, sir. Bearing zero,
          zero.

A flipping object on sonar screen.

                    SONAR OPERATOR
                    (continuing)
          It's zigzagging. Flipping end
          over end!

Object sinks to bottom of sonar screen.

                         SONAR OPERATOR
                          (continuing)
                 I don't know where it is now.

                        CAPTAIN FUNGITIS
                 It's sitting on the bottom.

Fungitis, itchy to shoot, twiddles his fingers.

                        CAPTAIN FUNGITIS
                          (continuing)
                 Load a skim-T torpedo.

                         VOICE (V.O.)
                        (from intercom)
                 S.T. torpedo ready, sir.

Sonar operator downloads coordinates into fire control
computer. Computer monitor reports, "Skim-T armed. Bow tube
#1. Ready. Are you sure?"

                        CAPTAIN FUNGITIS
                 Fire!

SWOOSH! Torpedo leaves. Crew waits silently. Fire control
computer tracks torpedo. Red dot moves across the sonar
screen as it tracks.

BACK TO SCENE

SAMUEL inches from the BIKER. Something snags Samuel. Biker
hollers,

                           BIKER
                 Shark!

SAMUEL'S POV

Rushing quickly to shore.

WIDER VIEW

Samuel rides the Skim-T torpedo to beach. He looks like
Tarzan, stabs it with his knife. Metallic pings as blade
strikes metal. Torpedo slides onto beach.

Samuel's flipped off. Torpedo scrapes parking lot under
parked cars, crosses street barely misses a tour bus full of
GRANDPAS. Sign on bus, "Eligible Bachelors."

Torpedo crosses sidewalk, slides up front steps of a home,
crashes through front door.

After a beat, SCREAMS radiate from the house KABOOM! Front
and sidewalls of the house collapse. Rear wall stands. Smoke
clears.

GOODMAN and FEMALES stand, clothes in tattered remnants. Goodman wears pink night robe, blue fluffy pompom slippers singed and smoldering.

He sees SAMUEL on beach. Samuel waves friendly-like. Goodman slices finger under his throat. SIRENS o.s.

Cop cars screech rubber on arrival. Goodman points finger to Samuel, COPS pursue. Samuel runs along beach out of view.

EXT. LONG BEACH / RESIDENTIAL AREA - DAY

SAMUEL hops through back yards, jumps fences, puts on bits of ladies clothes from clotheslines as he goes.

EXT. DOWNTOWN / LONG BEACH - DAY

SAMUEL'S dressed as a woman, walks barefoot. SHOPPERS giggle. A 5-year old BOY whacks his big toe with a plastic toy hammer OUCH!

Boy's MOTHER laughs. Samuel limps away. MAN extends $20 bill to Samuel.

                    MAN
          I need some love, sweetie.

Samuel slaps his hand, takes the $20 and runs.

SARAH with BULLDOG sees Samuel. She speaks MOS in a walkie-talkie.

INT. LIONFISH - DAY

CREW cheers. FUNGITIS confident and proud. SONAR OPERATOR gazes into computer monitor, scratches his head. His head blocks our view.

                    SONAR OPERATOR
          Captain, look at this.

Fungitis peers into the monitor.

                    CAPTAIN FUNGITIS
          Sure about this?

                    SONAR OPERATOR
          Diagnostics indicates systems
          functional.

                    CAPTAIN FUNGITIS
          Let's get outta here, fast!

Sonar Operator leaves his chair.

ON MONITOR

"Satlink com confirms offshore destruction of target."

INT. SUBMARINE - DAY

BERTHA looks in periscope, observes splintered pier and wood
fragments floating on a calm sea.

BIKERS row a boat, rescue others.

Bertha sees a commotion at Goodman's destroyed home.

                    BERTHA
          Down periscope. Full dive.

                    LANKY
          What's wrong?

                    BERTHA
          Mayor's house is demolished.

                    LANKY
          I'd say that's good.

                    BERTHA
          We fired one torpedo and we hit a
          boat. Who blew up the house?

                    LANKY
          Call Margaret.

                    CREW MEMBER
          Don't bother.

MARGARET'S angry face on computer monitor. Her expression
says it all.

INT. MAYOR'S OFFICE / CITY HALL - DAY

State of emergency meeting with SNITCH, SPINY, BIG DADDY and
SPIKE. GOODMAN's so upset hot steam vapors rise from his
face.

                    GOODMAN
                 (screaming)
          My yacht is blown up, my house
          demolished, and not one of you
          knows who did it?

With a sweep of both hands he knocks all papers, pens,
telephone, and two-way intercom from his desk to floor. Big
Daddy hands him a thin #10 envelope.

                    BIG DADDY
          Here's what we recovered.

>   GOODMAN
>   Get it out of my face!

Goodman slaps envelope. Money floats to floor.

>   SPIKE
>   Look, we're all in this together.
>   Let's cut the bullpoop.

Goodman calms, but still upset.

>   GOODMAN
>   That bonehead janitor. He's
>   working for the grannies.

>   SNITCH
>   Hardly. We tapped his phone and
>   tailed him. He's had no direct
>   contact with grannies.

>   GOODMAN
>   He's slick. He tells me things
>   yet never delivers evidence. He
>   was there! I saw him when my
>   house blew up. The grannies are
>   trying to kill me. He's a double
>   agent.

>   SNITCH
>   It's coincidence. He's an
>   authentic loser.

Noisy crowd outside on the front steps of City Hall. Goodman
peers out window, sees the MEDIA.

>   GOODMAN
>   Bloodthirsty vultures.

>   SNITCH
>   You must face them. They know it
>   was your home, your boat --

Goodman shakes fist at Snitch.

>   GOODMAN
>   And I'm going to tell them about
>   our little granny problem.
>   (disgusted)
>   Those darn grannies!

>   SNITCH
>   They won't buy that.

Goodman in Snitch's face.

                        GOODMAN
            Don't tell me what they will or
            will not buy. And with your damn
            lies, were going to pull it off.

Goodman waves his hands, they huddle in a circle.

                        GOODMAN
                      (continuing)
            Okay, here's the plan --

Desktop intercom on floor. Red light on listen mode.

INT. GOODMAN'S RECEPTION AREA - DAY

MRS. CRABAPPLE, listens to intercom, hand cupped to ear,
fingers over mouth, eyebrows twitch.

INT. PENTAGON / ADMIRAL'S OFFICE - DAY

ADMIRAL KAPOOCHI sits at desk surrounded by foxy WAVES. His
face smeared with pizza and lipstick. Waves can't keep their
hands off him. His shirt unbuttoned down to his bloated navel.

On the wall - POSTER, SAILOR peeks through keyhole of ladies
restroom. A big red X across the poster. Caption reads,
"The navy will not tolerate sexual harassment."

NAVAL OFFICER barges into room. Teletype message in hand.

                        NAVAL OFFICER
            Admiral Kapoochi, sir.

Kapoochi, shocked by the Officer's unannounced entry, rises
slowly, acts as nothing out of the ordinary happened, wipes
pizza sauce from lips onto sleeve.

                        KAPOOCHI
                      (calmly)
            Did you receive my message?

                        NAVAL OFFICER
            Message? Which message? Sir.

                        ADMIRAL KAPOOCHI
            I invited you to share pizza with
            me and my lovely assistants.

                        NAVAL OFFICER
            Oh, ah, me? Really?

                        ADMIRAL KAPOOCHI
            I most certainly did.

Waves smile with flirtatious eyes. Officer definitely
interested, but pulls himself together. He salutes.

                         NAVAL OFFICER
            Admiral, sir. Lionfish executed
            an unauthorized launch.

                         KAPOOCHI
                         (rapidly)
            Who? What? Where? When? How? Why?

Officer hands over teletype message. Kapoochi turns his back
to the officer. As he walks to phone, he crumples teletype
in hand, lifts handle on white telephone labeled, "White
House."

                         KAPOOCHI
                    (continuing; on phone)
            You get Lionfish to San Diego
            right likely now. There'll be
            purgatory to pay for this.

Slams phone so violently it shatters, then stuffs entire
pizza slice in mouth, garbles all to leave. Waves and
Officer quietly exit.

WAVE hurries back in, grabs shoes, casually strolls out,
barefoot, hugs shoes in arms, leaves door open.

Admiral's SECRETARY (68) sits just outside the door, sees
wave exit.

Secretary sees Kapoochi grasp head in hands, mumbles to his
pizza pie. She gets up and closes the door.

Secretary dials a number on phone.

INT. CITY HALL / AUDITORIUM - DAY

GOODMAN interviews NEWS MEDIA, TV cameras, REPORTERS,
PHOTOGRAPHERS. SNITCH snuggles behind Goodman.

                         REPORTER
            Mr. Mayor, are terrorist involved?
            You the target? Why?

                         GOODMAN
            Funding is insufficient to
            maintain basic services. I have
            contacted Governor --

                         REPORTER
            We know all about that. We want
            to know why your boat and your
            home was destroyed. What gives?

Goodman's eyes flinch nervously. Snitch frowns.

                              GOODMAN
                    It's a conspiracy to discredit my
                    reputation. Last month I played
                    bingo. I won twice. The grannies
                    didn't like that. They threatened
                    me. I didn't think anything of it,
                    until --

                              ANOTHER REPORTER
                    You expect your constituents to
                    believe that muck and slime story?

                              GOODMAN
                    It's true, we have proof. Hard
                    evidence.

Snitch displays six evidence bags. Places them on podium. He
picks up a plastic bag labeled, "Evidence #CU47-K"

                              SNITCH
                    A sampling of one-hundred items
                    retrieved from the crime scene.
                    As you can see --

He flicks away burnt fragments of paper, holds them high.
So many photographer strobe lights flash, Snitch appears in
slow motion.

                              SNITCH
                         (continuing)
                    Our bomb squad verifies powder
                    burns on this paper to be
                    identical to the chemical
                    signature used in the bomb which
                    blew up the Mayor's yacht.

                              ANOTHER REPORTER
                    Anyone can buy gunpowder at any
                    dozen gun stores. How does this
                    tie in with grannies?

Snitch dangles burnt pieces of paper.

                              SNITCH
                    Bomb fragments. Disposable bingo
                    paper.

INT. MARGARET'S LIVING ROOM - DAY

MARGARET in rocking chair knits a sock, eyes TV news. She's
disturbed, fidgety. Her black granny shoe taps the floor.
FLUFFY curled on her lap.

ON TV

SNITCH reveals another plastic bag dangling from fingertips.
Label reads, "Evidence #ICUP-K"

                    SNITCH (V.O.)
          These bomb fragments taken from
          the Mayor's house. Shrapnel
          inside the bomb. Sewing
          paraphernalia.

WIDER VIEW

MARGARET leans forward as SNITCH on TV reveals powder burned
pins, needles, thimbles, and cheap costume jewelry.
Margaret's extremely upset, shoe raps hard.

ON TV

                    SNITCH (V.O.)
          These items are typical of a
          senior citizen would use to make
          a bomb. Crime statistics reveal
          patterns of people who make
          homemade bombs will use items they
          are most familiar with. As you can
          see, truly items a granny would
          use.

                    FEMALE REPORTER (V.O.)
          Do the powderburn signatures match?

                    SNITCH (V.O.)
          Yes.

GOODMAN smiles. TV cameras focus on him.

                    GOODMAN (V.O.)
          Crime is out of control. The
          nature of the times we live in.
          It is the beast in mankind.

REPORTERS all ask questions simultaneously. Goodman raises
hand, motions to crowd to let him continue.

                    GOODMAN (V.O.)
                    (continuing)
          We live in a dangerous world. I
          tell you all, I am committed all
          in my power to take back our
          beloved city!

WIDER VIEW

MARGARET stands, holds FLUFFY by the TV, her hand on chin in
deep concentration. Sun drifts. Margaret clicks on a lamp.
Anchorman TOM BROKER comments,

                    TOM BROKER (V.O.)
          Good evening, I'm Tom Broker.
          Lost Angus is under attack by
          terrorist grannies.
                    (beat)
          Our crime problem is appalling.
          Devastating our economy. The
          perpetual riot-induced fires
          transform the inversion layer. The
          air is intolerable to breathe.
          Industry is leaving taking
          thousands of jobs from our youth.
                    (beat)
          Lost Angus, overridden with
          criminals is crumbling to its
          knees.

The phone rings.

                    MARGARET
                    (on phone)
          Yes. I know. I know about that.
          What? How was I supposed to know
          a nuclear sub was patrolling?
          That's your job.
                    (beat)
          No, sir. I'm tired. Yes, sir.
          Thank you, sir. Good... night.

Margaret slams phone, mumbles under her breath. She clicks
off TV, takes FLUFFY upstairs to bed.

JENNIFER enters front door dressed as a movie star with six
drunken SAILORS. She holds a jewel-studded mirror. Adoringly
gazes into her reflection.

EXT. VARIOUS LOCATIONS - NIGHT

SERIES OF SHOTS

- - SPINY places box of wood matches on windowsill of Lost
Angus Senior Citizens Bingo Parlor. Inserts lit cigarette
into book of matches, slips assembly into box of wood
matches, dashes away.

MOMENTS LATER

Flames erupt. SPINY and HOMEBOYS across the street by the
"Greasy Boy" hot dog stand laugh.

- - BIG DADDY and SAD DEVIL'S GANG slip dynamite on all four sides of the Heavenly Hills Senior Citizens Center. They ride away on. Big Daddy, electronically detonates the charge KABOOM!

- - SPIKE and L.A. COWBOY'S GANG blast interior of a Bingo Hall with shotguns, revolvers.

One has an old flintlock pistol. Hall torched with gasoline.

- - LOST ANGUS POLICE cars roam the streets, tell GRANNIES on cruiser PA systems, "All grannies, get out of town." Black GRANNY, SAPPHIRE (66) hurls a tube of lipstick at cruiser, splatters red wax on side window. COPS chase her on foot down the sidewalk.

INT. DEPARTMENT STORE / MENS RESTROOM - NIGHT

They corner SAPPHIRE in a stall. COPS peek under stalls. Her black granny shoes give her away.

They pry open door. She wallops them with pocketbook, slams the stall door shut.

Sapphire cracks open the door, wiggles her finger to invite a COP inside. Cop enters. He sails over the top of the door. Cops rip door off hinges, charge inside, but Sapphire isn't there.

They look under stalls and see no shoes. They hear a toilet flush. They go to the stall, barge in, see Sapphire standing on toilet pipe. One shoe on the flush valve.

She has a pouting look on her face.

INT. CORINNE'S HOME / LIVING ROOM - NIGHT

PENELOPE and CORINNE watch soap opera, "As The Earth Ages."

On TV - ELIZABETH (75) leaps onto a bed sobbing. MILDRED (88) comforts her.

                    ELIZABETH (V.O.)
          Frank told me its over. He's
          seeing another woman. It's
          Jeanette! Mildred, what am I to do?

Elizabeth again bursts into tears. Mildred sits on side of bed tenderly wipes away Elizabeth's tears.

                    MILDRED (V.O.)
          Elizabeth, there are many crabs in
          the sea. You'll find another.

                    ELIZABETH (V.O.)
          But I love him.

WIDER VIEW

CORINNE and PENELOPE extremely angry.

                    CORINNE
          Jeanette is Frank's nurse! That
          no good two timing --

EXT. HOLLYWOOD / SUNSET STRIP - NIGHT

SAD DEVILS gang cruise Sunset Strip past Vine street on
Harley Davidsons. SPECTATORS gawk as they thunder by. BIG
DADDY and MAD DOG in front row side-by-side.

SARAH follows SAMUEL on sidewalk, she throws banana. Samuel
bends down, picks up penny. Banana smacks a BIKER in last
row in the face. Biker falls off Harley, lands on hood of
parked cop car.

INT. COP CAR - NIGHT

Lazy COP eats a donut, reaches out, snaps handcuffs to the
BIKER and side mirror.

EXT. STREET / BY COP CAR - NIGHT

SARAH spanks BIKER with her cane.

                    SARAH
          Repent, sinful child, repent.

Biker smiles. BULLDOG bites leg. Biker screams. SAMUEL
sees the activity, slips away.

EXT. HOLLYWOOD / SUNSET STRIP - NIGHT

BIG DADDY and SPIKE'S motorcycle gang rumble down the street.

                    BIG DADDY
          Mad Dog, you know we gotta get the
          Mayor's money back.

                    MAD DOG
          Yeah, but how ya gonna do it Big
          Daddy?

Mad Dog guns throttle, pulls wheelie for the crowd.

                    BIG DADDY
          Easy. Spiny's gonna make a drop
          Sunday in Santa Monica. He drops,
          we lift!

                    MAD DOG
          Too risky. Goodman will kill us
          if he finds out.

They giggle like little girls as they pull in to Mann's
Chinese Theater. The movie, "Grandfather Takes On The
Congressional Mob." Poster reveals old man (88) in black
leathers firing a Gatling gun at politicians.

Big Daddy slips off his bike, approaches three BLACK
TEENAGERS in line near ticket booth. The teenagers vibrate
in fear.

> BIG DADDY
> How would you gentlemen like to
> make $500 each tomorrow? I don't
> take no very easily.

Teenagers readily agree.

JANET (80) inside ticket booth increases volume on window
speaker. She's dressed like a spy.

INT. CAR - NEXT DAY

SPINY and three HOMEBOYS in a low rider Lincoln Continental.
Spiny in front seat. A wannabe gang member LITTLE HEART (12)
drives.

Car bounces erratically, tires screech as Little Heart pumps
gas pedal and slams the brakes repeatedly. Spiny's impressed,
winks eye at Little Heart.

> SPINY
> (to Homeboys)
> Hey, get a load of Little Heart.
> He's got it down!

Little Heart smiles ear-to-ear. Spiny stares at him. No
smile.

> SPINY
> (continuing)
> You gonna do good for your
> homeboys today. No screwup, you
> understand? Pull over and park
> right there.

EXT. SANTA MONICA VISTA - DAY

LITTLE HEART'S serious, as macho as a twelve year old can.
He parks in street by the Vista that overlooks the beach and
Highway 1.

All eyes scan the area.

INT. CAR - DAY

HOMEBOY in back seat retrieves paper bag under seat. SPINY
takes it, looks inside, appears satisfied. He tosses bag on
LITTLE HEART'S lap.

                    SPINY
                (to Little Heart)
          This is it. Once you do this
          you're in for life. You can back
          out now and we'll take you home to
          your mama.

                (beat)
          You think hard. You may end up in
          prison with your uncle, your
          cousins, your school chums. Nobody
          but you can make that decision.

Little Heart looks sad. He sees,

A FLEETING VISION - DAY

LITTLE HEART's GRANDMOTHER drags him into the house by the
earlobe.

                    GRANDMOTHER
          Stay away from those gangs, they
          will take you to hell!

BACK TO SCENE / VISION ENDS

                    SPINY
                (impatient)
          Get in the back seat. Taking you
          home to mummy.

LITTLE HEART twiddles earlobe, steps out of car.

EXT. CAR - DAY

Back door creaks opens, GANG MEMBER steps out, meanly looks
LITTLE HEART in the eye.

                    GANG MEMBER
          You got little heart, Little Heart.

Little Heart shoves the laughing gang member away.

                    LITTLE HEART
          Gimme the bag.

Gang members remain silent.

                    SPINY
          Under the park bench.

Little Heart fast-steps to bench, places bag, returns to car, tries to act cool. SPINY dangles car keys. Little Heart takes the key, Spiny won't let go.

                    SPINY
                 (continuing)
            You just ruined your life, homeboy.

Spiny smiles, lets go of the key.

INT. CAR - DAY

They wait. HOMEBOY in back seat slaps LITTLE HEART'S shoulder. Little Heart cranks out a half-smile as he fondles his ear lobe.

The three BLACK TEENAGERS approach park bench. They see the bag and sit down.

CHARLIE reaches under bench, retrieves bag. They all get up, walk away.

SPINY sees the drop is good. Little Heart drives away, all smiles, bounces the Lincoln as they go.

COP CAR flashes lights, SIREN wails. Little Heart stomps the gas.

EXT. PARKING LOT / SANTA MONICA VISTA - DAY

Six GRANNIES dressed in motercycle gang colors, approach the three BLACK TEENAGERS. PENELOPE leads the pack. MARGARET in b.g. on a thumping Harley chopper.

CHARLIE holds moneybag.

                    PENELOPE
                 (deep man's voice)
            Turn it over. Good job. We'll
            take it from here.

CHARLIE hugs bag close to chest.

                    CHARLIE
            We were told to drop it. No one
            said you would arrive. Since when
            do geezers ride with gangs?

                    PENELOPE
            Big Daddy has a change of plans.
            He will meet you back at the
            theater. Tomorrow, eight p.m.
            That's when you get paid your five-
            hundred dollars.

Reluctantly, Charlie hands bag to Penelope. SAMUEL disguised as a wino leans under a palm tree, sips Papaya Tango wine.

As the grannies thunder off on Harley's, he follows in an old rust bucket station wagon, all rust, no paint on this vehicle anywhere. Plenty of body rot.

EXT. SANTA MONICA VISTA - DAY

SPIKE and his GANG arrive at picnic table, push PEOPLE aside, desperately search for money bag. Tear open PEDESTRIANS lunch bags.

                    SPIKE
          It's not here. Spiny ripped us
          off.

EXT. CHINESE MANN'S THEATER - EVENING

Three black TEENAGERS stand in line to see movie, "How The West Was Ruined." They appear agitated.

JANET in ticket booth slips them tickets.

                    CHARLIE
               (to his friends)
          Man, those geezers sure were rowdy
          looking weren't they?

Teenagers enter theater. Janet resets time schedule back 1/2 hour to 8 p.m.

BIG DADDY and his GANG arrive, look around, panic.

                    BIG DADDY
          We've been ripped off!

Janet smiles.

INT. HEAVENLY HILLS HOTEL - NIGHT

GOODMAN hosts the, "Annual Railroad Crowning of the Bums Pageant."

SNITCH behind stage curtain, periodically peeks.

                    GOODMAN
          Gentlemen, I am honored to be here
          with you tonight.

Drunken crowd of BUMS applaud.

Some steal cans of canned-heat tray warming jelly from banquet table, strain it into wine glasses.

Label on can reads, Danger poison. "Do not swig, sip, gulp,
devour, swill, guzzle, engorge, pour down throat, or place in
wine glass."

                    GOODMAN
                (continuing)
        Thank you. Thank you very much.
        Living on the rails is not for the
        meek. It is an American
        tradition. I am proud of your
        courage. The city of Lost Angus
        welcomes you.

                    BUMS CHANTING
        Crown the King. Crown the King.

                    GOODMAN
        And now, I present to you, the
        King of Bums.

Goodman extends hand. Drunken BUM staggers to stage with
envelope. Crowd silent. Goodman tears envelope.

                    GOODMAN
                (continuing)
        The King is, Bobby Pimplehead!

Bums applaud, howl like lonely coyotes. BOBBY PIMPLEHEAD
drinks a quart of jelly, a pure wreck.

They physically carry him onto stage, hold him up as Goodman
places a gold crown on his head.

Crowd cheers as he cradles roses in his arms.

Snitch pokes head from curtain, motions frantically to
Goodman.

Goodman approaches, but he's embarrassed and tries to
apologize so as not to offend the bums at this critical
highlight of the Pageant.

                    GOODMAN
                (continuing)
        What do you want? This better be
        important or you'll be Queen of
        the bums in one-minute.

Snitch grabs Goodman's arm, pulls him slightly behind curtain.

                    SNITCH
        We got a problem, Mayor. The
        money's gone!

                    GOODMAN
        What? What?

                         SNITCH
              Spiny made the drop. He said L.A.
              Cowboy's picked up the dough as
              planned. Spike claims his guys
              made the pick up, but the loot
              wasn't there.

                         GOODMAN
              You mean to tell me I just lost
              six million dollars? That does
              it. I'm not playing any more games!

INT. MAYOR OFFICE - NEXT DAY, MORNING

GOODMAN meets with SPINY and his HOMEBOYS. Phone rings.
Goodman speaks into intercom.

                         GOODMAN
              Mayor, Goodman. How may I help
              you today?

SPLIT SCREEN

EXT. BUSY CITY STREET / SAMUEL IN PHONE BOOTH - DAY

No door on phone booth. SAMUEL cups hand to ear to shield
noise.

KID on a dirt bike backs up, points tailpipe at Samuel YING!
YING! YING!

Blue smoke pours into phone booth. Samuel gags, pinches his
nose as he speaks into phone.

                         SAMUEL
              Mr. Mayor? It is Samuel. Please
              don't hang up. I know who's got
              the money and I can lead you to
              them. You still mad at me?

                         GOODMAN
                    (on phone)
              Samuel, you skinny old rat. My
              old buddy. Where have you been?
              I miss you.

Samuel kicks at the kid on the dirt bike, but his foot jams
in the rear wheel spokes.

Kid smirks as he slowly releases clutch, squeezes Samuel's
foot OUCH!

Samuel wiggles free. Kid leaves him in a haze of blue smoke.

>   SAMUEL
> Hello? Hello? Mayor Goodman? I'm
> hiding from the cops you sent
> after me. Remember?

Another KID presses receiver lever, runs away laughing. Dial tone. Samuel throws rock, misses, splashes a parked car windshield. He redials phone.

>   GOODMAN
> Why don't you have lunch with me
> and we'll talk about it, okay?

>   SAMUEL
> No tricks?

Another KID faces his boom box to Samuel's nose.

>   GOODMAN
> No tricks. Meet me at MuChacho's
> bar at one O'clock.

>   SAMUEL
> That's a gay bar!

>   GOODMAN
> Safest place I know and not get
> harassed by the ladies.

>   SAMUEL
> No way. Let's go to McBrutal's.

SARAH in b.g. with BULLDOG hands the kids lollipops, money and Granny Apples.

INT. 49'ER SALOON / ACTON - DAY

SPIKE and his gang sit silently with sad puppy dog expressions.

Roar of Harley's pull into parking lot o.s.

BIG DADDY swings open door, stands silent, looks mean. Spike, scared, cautiously approaches Big Daddy.

>   SPIKE
> We didn't do it.

Big Daddy doesn't say anything, stares grimly.

>   SPIKE
>   (continuing)
> I swear, we didn't do it. We were
> set up. We're not the ones.

Big Daddy snaps fingers, his GANG enters with shotguns held
close to their legs, barrels to floor.

Spike, visibly shaken, approaches Big Daddy. Spike falls
hard to his knees.

                    SPIKE
               (continuing)
          Please! Please! Listen to me.
          We'll give you our bikes, our club
          house, our old girlfriends. Okay?
          Just don't kill us, man.
               (hopefully)
          We can work it out. Yes?

Big Daddy stares down on Spike, tears flood Spikes cheeks.
Spike grasps Big Daddy's boots.

Big Daddy takes two steps back, leaves Spike on his knees.
Spike looks up to Big Daddy like a sad puppy.

                    BIG DADDY
               (with authority)
          Get up and die like a man.

MAD DOG and another BIKER lift Spike to his feet.

Big Daddy slips Bowie knife from boot, places tip under
Spikes eye. Tears drip onto the gold plated blade.

                    BIG DADDY
               (continuing; harsh)
          I told you not to step on my toes.
               (yells)
          Where's the money?

                    SPIKE
               (slobbering)
          I don't know. I swear. We didn't
          take it, cross ma'heart and hope
          to --

Big Daddy grabs Spike by hair, pulls him closer to blade tip.
Spike resists, but Mad Dog has a good hold on him by the ears.

Mad Dog giggles, his single tooth flashes.

                    MAD DOG
          Cut him. I hate thieves.

                    SPIKE
          Please, Big Daddy. Killing me
          won't get the money back.

                        MAD DOG
               Stick it in his eye and watch him
               die!

Big Daddy calmly places folded piece of paper into Spike's
pocket.

Big Daddy wraps fist around knife, pulls it back high over
his shoulder like a tightly wound spring.

Spike's horrified, lips quiver, hands folded in prayer.

                        BIG DADDY
                    (coldly)
               Okay, everyone get up. Stand by
               the bar.
                    (to Spike)
               You too!

Spike's gang twist their bodies tightly against bar. Some
cover their face with forearms. Big Daddy and Mad Dog step
back.

Double-barrel shotguns rise to hip level. Hammers click to
full-cock position KA-BOOM! KA-BOOM!

White snowy objects soar from muzzles, pelt bikers with a
vengeance. Gang scatters out door. Start bikes.

Victims realize it's only popcorn, dash outside.

EXT. BIKER BAR - DAY

L.A. Cowboy's chase Sad Devils on foot whom ride away
laughing in the wind.

SPIKE removes note from pocket. It reads, "You're clean this
time. We need $6 mil to pay you know who. Do what's
necessary."

EXT. STREET - DAY

SPIKE and his gang ride like maniacs. Some on sidewalks knock
over trash cans. Some spin wheels into neighbors pristine
lawns.

BIKER rides top of parked cars, windshields implode, hoods
crumple. NEIGHBORS scream.

Dogs run, but a CAT pursues, chases Spike down the street.
Cat attacks, leaps on Spike's back, clawing.

Spike tumbles off bike, runs. Cat leaps on his leg, digs in
claws and teeth. More CATS arrive, encircle Spike, snarling
and hissing with flashing teeth.

                         SPIKE
               Pssss! Back off, kitties. I'm
               warning you. Pssss!

They leap. Spike screams.

EXT. WOODLAND HILLS / ULMUS DRIVE - DAY

L.A. COWBOYS gang solicit an upscale residential
neighborhood, rap on doors. Each holds donation can with a
picture of SPIKE wearing his colors in a wheelchair.

Caption on cans reads, "Help him ride again!"

When they ask for a donation, ELDERLY HOMEOWNERS can't say
no. BIKER stands by their car with sledge hammer.

After a few cars get whacked, homeowners write checks and
deposit them into the cans.

WOODLAND HILLS / MALL PARKING LOT - DAY

SAMUEL spies from rusty station wagon. MARGARET, PENELOPE,
CORINNE stand by a white stretch limousine.

SARAH lets air out of Samuel's rear tire. BULLDOG chews on
other rear tire.

INT. LIMOUSINE - DAY

Six excited GRANNIES in military combat fatigues apply black
and green camouflage makeup to faces. DEBBIE in drivers
seat. LOLITA and JANET in front seat. DONNA in back seat.

                         MARGARET
               Show 'em grandma knows best.

Grannies whoop and holler and off they go.

Samuel tries to follow, but flat tires stop him. SARAH with
BULLDOG stroll by. She hums a tune.

EXT. TOPANGA CANYON ROAD - DAY

GRANNIES in limo pass two red traffic lights. Armored car
overturns. PEOPLE scramble for money scattered in street.
Chasing money creates traffic havoc.

Grannies turn left almost at top of hill. They take second
left to Ulmus Drive, continue to apply makeup to their faces.

EXT. WOODLAND HILLS / ULMUS DRIVE - DAY

ATTACK SEQUENCE

FIRST PASS - GRANNIES sit on windowsills, shoot the
motorcycles, chrome parts shatter like glass. Firepower so
intense bikes pushed along the ground. Flash grenades hurled
blind the bikers BOOM! BOOM!

SPIKE watches from down the street, sees limousine come right
at him. Hops his Harley, drives between two homes, escapes.
Grannies skid around the block.

SECOND PASS - Bikers pick up their bikes, grannies open fire.
Bikers fall faster than leaves in a wind storm. Motorcycles
break up from rubber bullet impacts.

Grannies step out of limo, take sniper positions, pick off
limping stragglers. Cease fire. Bikers roll on lawns,
whimper like children.

GRANNIES and GRANDPAS exit homes, cheer the GI's. Some
grannies spank injured bikers with canes. One granny pokes
hers torturously into a BIKER'S sore knee. Others retrieve
donation cans.

MOMENTS LATER

SIRENS o.s. GRANNIES burn rubber. COP CAR blocks path.
Grannies fishtail a pristine lawn, escape.

EXT. TOPANGA CANYON - DAY

GRANNIES race down Topanga Canyon, miss a turn, fly off a
canyon gorge. SCREAMS fill the air as trunk of car descends
cliff. KABOOM! Puff of smoke rises.

COP with gun drawn peers over edge, sees grannies parachutes
snared in trees. Car burns in ravine. Reaches for portable
radio, hesitates.

                    COP
                 (to himself)
            Oh no, the guys will never let me
            off knowing grandmothers outran
            me. This never happened.

Cop steps into car, takes off down the hill.

MARGARET steps out of her Rolls Royce, looks over ridge, sees
the mess. Grannies below call for help.

                         MARGARET
                    (to the grannies)
               I'm not going down there. There's
               rattlesnakes in that canyon. I'll
               send for help.

The grannies faces droop, eyes search for snakes.

EXT. TOPANGA CANYON RAVINE - DAY

GRANNIES parachutes entangled in trees, they hopelessly sway
in the breeze. With green faces and black bands around their
eyes they look like raccoons, hands drooped like begging
puppies.

HOWL o.s. of distant hound dogs. DOGS arrive. They're
FRENCH POODLES, but they sound like hound dogs.

Chain saw engine buzzes o.s. SAMUEL in hunting outfit and
backpack exits from dense brush with chain saw idling in hand.

                         SAMUEL
               Come on down ladies, or I'll cut
               you down. One-by-one.

Samuel cuts trees. Grannies tumble out. He hooks them into
a chain gang and out they go.

INT. MC'BRUTAL'S RESTAURANT - DAY

SAMUEL and GOODMAN gulp hot dogs by candlelight in a fast
food eatery. Samuel's toilet plunger on table.

                         SAMUEL
               I even got this photograph for
               evidence. I hope they rot in jail.

Samuel hands Goodman a photo of granny bikers taking money
from a brown paper bag. Goodman smiles.

                         GOODMAN
               Good work, Sam. Where's the money?

                         SAMUEL
               I don't know, Mr. Goodman. I lost
               them on the Ventura freeway. The
               grannies I captured won't talk.
               Maybe the jailhouse guards have
               the money?

Goodman crumples photo in fist. Sam spills coffee to floor.

FAT LADY with tray of food slips on coffee, tumbles down on
Goodman OUCH! Food falls, plasters their faces.

SARAH with BULLDOG sit in a booth. MANAGER arrives, tells
Sarah to leave. She whacks his knee with cane. Bulldog
leaps on him, tears his shirt. He runs.

Lady grabs Goodman and Samuel's collar, pushes them out the
exit. Sarah and bulldog follow, she speaks in walkie-talkie.

                    SARAH
               Mebom one, I've got the dips on
               'em. Over.

Lady beats up Goodman and Samuel. PEOPLE gather, cheer,
place bets. Sarah smiles, places a bet.

INT. JAIL - DAY

GOODMAN and SAMUEL walk a cell block, look into Cell #117,
see the captured GRANNIES inside dressed in gray and white
striped prison attire.

DEBBIE, LOLITA, JANET, DONNA and SAPPHIRE inside cell.
Donna's short and thin, but with her enormous weight-lifting
arms she appears deformed.

                    GOODMAN
               Well, well, well, look what we
               have here.

Donna reaches through bars, grabs Samuel's throat with an
ironclad grip, lifts him clear off the floor. Samuel swings
plunger, but drops it to floor.

Her arm looks like Arnold Schwarzenegger's with a tattoo of
Popeye eating spinach.

Samuel gasps air desperately, grips the arm that chokes him.
Goodman leaps from bars.

                    GOODMAN
                 (continuing)
               Help! Guard!

Burly GUARDS arrive, beat Donna's arm with PR-24 nightsticks
emitting a sickening painful sound. Donna laughs.

                    DONNA
               I was only having a little fun.

                    GOODMAN
               Who are you? Who hired you? What
               is it you want? Talk to me.

Debbie approaches grill. Goodman checks his distance.

                         DEBBIE
              You took our city and we want it
              back.

                         GOODMAN
                      (chuckling)
              A few little grannies? Hardly a
              threat!

Guards laugh. Samuel rubs his throat.

                         DEBBIE
              You haven't seen nothing yet.
              Just wait until, Margaret --

                         GOODMAN
              Margaret?

Debbie say's no more, sits in corner of cell. Goodman,
Samuel and guards rush to,

INT. CONTROL ROOM - DAY

GOODMAN on phone.

                         GOODMAN
              Bingo! We got'em, Snitch. The
              leader's name is Margaret.

                         SNITCH (V.O.)
              That's all I need to know.

Goodman rewardingly pats SAMUEL on head, hands him a cookie.
Samuel eats as he buffs his plunger with arm.

INT. CORINNE'S HOME / LIVING ROOM - DAY

CORINNE watches Soap Opera, "As The Earth Ages."

MILK COMMERCIAL ON TV

Three 90-year old MEN in diapers at the beach cradled in arms
of beautiful bikini-clad teenage VALLEY GIRLS feeding them
milk with baby bottles. Bumper reads, "Milk Makes Dreams
Come True."

TV COMMERCIAL ENDS

In corner of room, a velvet cape covers a huge object.
Corinne prances to it, pokes finger inside.

                         CORINNE
              Hello my love. Are you hungry?

Cape sways.

> VOICE (V.O.)
> (parrot voice)
> Awk! Granny's good looking.

Corinne opens cape, reveals a enormous VULTURE in a cage.
Corinne places a fat brown rat inside, closes the cape. Cage
rattles, shakes, then a beat of silence. GULP! BURP!

Corinne reclines on couch, sips a can of, "Healthy Bowels
Fiber Punch."

ON TV

JEANETTE (60) enters front door of a house.

SUSAN (65) in living room.

> SUSAN (V.O.)
> Who are you?

> JEANETTE (V.O.)
> Who am I? Who are you? And what
> are you doing here in my house?

> SUSAN (V.O.)
> Your house? I'm Frank's fiancee!

Corinne sits on edge of couch absorbed by the scandal.

ON TV

SUSAN and JEANETTE stand in silent rage. They look hard at
an OLD MAN in a wheelchair.

It's FRANK. He wears a white jonnie. His mouth drooped wide,
eye's half-closed, comatose, oblivious of anything happening
around him.

WIDER VIEW

> CORINNE
> You beastly man of infidelity.
> You two-timing no good... how
> could you do this to Jeanette?
> She loved you.

Corinne angrily rises to her feet, face to Frank.

> CORINNE
> (continuing)
> Debbie was right. You never had
> hemorrhoids did you?

Ticker tape message runs across bottom of TV screen, "News
brief. Drive-by shooting in Woodland Hills. Grannies
arrested. Evening news at 5 p.m. Channel 6."

Corinne scrambles to telephone, punches digits so hard the
key pad squeals for mercy.

SPLIT SCREEN / CORINNE AND MARGARET ON PHONE

                    CORINNE
          Margaret, did you see the news?
          Debbie and the girls are busted.

                    MARGARET
          How do you know this?

                    CORINNE
          It was on the soap opera.

                    MARGARET
          Corinne, how many times must we
          tell you the Soap's are not real?

FLUFFY leaps to Margaret's lap, sniffs phone.

                    CORINNE
          News brief flashed while I was
          watching Frank squirm his way out
          of his immoral activities --

                    MARGARET
          You sure?

                    CORINNE
          Honest, I've been faithfully
          taking my prune juice and I can
          think clearly now.

VULTURE hobbles across living room floor to kitchen.

                    MARGARET
          Oh Darn it! This is bad. Real
          bad news. We could lose
          everything. They'll convict our
          girls, Corinne. We're talking
          prison time.

                    CORINNE
          What can we do?

Margaret cradles Fluffy like a baby.

                    MARGARET
          Pick you up in ten minutes. Call
          Penelope. Tell her to go to
          yellow alert.

Both hang up. Sound of FLAPPING wings o.s. Pots and pans
sail out of Corinne's kitchen. Chair soars by, almost hits
Corinne, crashes on living room wall, knocks down dinosaur
dung collection.

                    CORINNE
               (to vulture)
          That does it. No ice cream for
          you tonight.

EXT. CORINNE'S HOUSE - DAY

MARGARET in her Rolls picks up CORINNE. They drive Pacific
Coast Highway to,

EXT. MALIBU / BY BEACH - DAY

They approach DON WONG'S restaurant. A huge flock of white
SEAGULLS soar the beach-side of the restaurant.

Sign reads, "Don Wong's exotic seafood. Happy hour all the
time."

                    CORINNE
          Oh, look! Doves.

                    MARGARET
          Those aren't doves Corinne,
          they're seagulls.

                    CORINNE
          Let's eat there. I want to watch
          the birds. Sure they're seagulls?
          Could be white crows.

INT. DON WONG'S RESTAURANT - DAY

MARGARET and CORINNE select beach-side window seat.

Out the window, CHILDREN play in the surf. PARENTS intently
watch children. Gulls soar by window.

LIFEGUARD surrounded with drooling GIRLS. He flexes as Mr.
America, skinny as a rail. Girls rub his exposed ribs with
suntan oil.

Asian WAITER arrives with pot of tea.

                    WAITER
          Ah, so sorry fo delay. Dumb
          busboy sick. He go home.

                    CORINNE
          Constipation? It's going around
          you know. Like the flu.

                         WAITER
               Busboy surf. I say no. Too
               danger. He no listen. Big shark
               bite him.

                         CORINNE
               You mean Jaws? He's here in
               Malibu?

                         WAITER
               You lookie out window you see him.

          Waiter slides open window, children play in the surf.

          Corinne and Margaret both point to the special on the menu,
          "Deep fried pelican webs in sea urchin sauce. Includes sand
          flea salad, yellow pee soup, tea and fortune cookie $12.95."

                         MARGARET
               We'll take the special, please.

          Waiter fumbles with his fly. Margaret picks up a fork, gives
          him a serious look. He leaves.

          Corinne pours tea that resembles thick chocolate syrup.

                         MARGARET
                    (continuing)
               What in grief is it?

                         CORINNE
               Black lagoon tea. It's the newest
               fad. Made from Mongolian
               toadstools.

                         MARGARET
               I hate mushrooms!

                         CORINNE
               They ain't mushrooms.

          Margaret recoils, sniffs the hot vapors, gags. Corinne sips
          and smiles. Pours some in Margaret's cup.

          Margaret lights a cigarette. Waiter enters back door, carries
          a squawking brown pelican into the kitchen.

          Margaret stares at him, snubs cigarette into black tea.
          Flames flash from the cup then die out.

                         CORINNE
                    (continuing)
               Methane gas.

          A commotion on the beach. Margaret and Corinne see screaming
          kid's dash to shore.

                    CORINNE
                 (continuing)
        Oh Margaret, look. There he is.
        It's Jaws!

A bar of MUSIC from "Jaws" movie.

JAW'S mouth wide-open, chases kids onto beach, then thrashes
his way into deep water. Kids scream with joy and rush right
back into the surf.

                    MARGARET
        What are those fool kids doing?

                    CORINNE
        Isn't it lovely? I tell you
        animals were made for children.
                 (squinting)
        They're just playing Margaret.

Chinese chime MUSIC plays, LOUDLY.

Margaret shields ears. Corinne taps fingers to music.

                    MARGARET
        Shut that bloody music down,
        please!

COOK'S head pokes from kitchen. He wears ear protection
muffs, smiles. MUSIC lowers.

Waiter delivers meal. Two black pelican webs stick straight
up out of the plate with sawed-off legs stuck in gooey yellow
sauce.

Margaret gags, shoves it away. Corinne digs in. Pelican
web bones crunch. Waiter closes curtain.

                    WAITER
                 (mumbling)
        You no need this. Upset digestion.

Bloodcurdling SCREAM o.s., shouts of hysteria.

                    KIDS (V.O.)
        He's got Billy! He's got Billy!
        Run!

                    A MOTHER (V.O.)
        That's enough! Get out of the
        water.

                    A FATHER (V.O.)
        Look out. Michael, he's right
        behind you!

                              KIDS (V.O.)
                         He's got Louise!

Margaret and Corinne stare at each other. Corinne has a
mouth full of food, wags her head. Margaret nods.

                              KIDS (V.O.)
                              (continuing)
                    Mommy! Daddy! Jaws is bad. He
                    don't like Billy.

                            LIFEGUARD (V.O.)
                    That's not Jaws. It's his mean
                    brother Jowls. He hates kids.
                    Out of the water.

Margaret slams window shut. Corinne nudges curtain aside to
peek outside. Margaret slaps her hand.

Waiter carries a stack of dirty plates, steps out back door,
lays plates on back deck, returns to kitchen.

Sound of wings flap and gulls cry loudly o.s.

Margaret opens curtain, see a flock of GULLS clean the plates
and JOWLS about to clamp his jaws onto some KID.

Margaret closes curtain, slams fork down onto table.

                              MARGARET
                    We got problems. Big problems.

Corinne gently places hand on Margaret's, then she stuffs a
pelican web in her mouth, rips a piece. Bones crunch as she
chews.

                              CORINNE
                    Eat, Margaret. I hear the food in
                    jail is very good these days.
                    They'll be okay.

Margaret in deep thought. PENELOPE enters.

INT. MILITARY COURT - DAY

Sentence phase of court-martial. CAPTAIN FUNGITIS stands.
JUDGE scans OFFICERS on jury bench.

                              JUDGE
                    Have you reached a verdict?

Each officer in turn rises, say's "Yes." Then sits,
reminding us of a fluid stack of dominoes.

The last OFFICER stands. She's a GRANNY.

                         JUDGE
                      (continuing)
              Well, is he guilty or what?

                         OFFICER
              The bum is guilty, sir!

                         JUDGE
                      (to Fungitis)
              I hereby find you guilty of
              inappropriate behavior in disgrace
              to the Navy. Captain Fungitis, do
              you wish to address the court?

                    CAPTAIN FUNGITIS
              Give me Liberty, or give me death!

Officers whisper to each other, nod heads in agreement to the
Judge. Judge slams gavel down WHACK!

                         JUDGE
              So be it. Tomorrow at the break
              of dawn. Lets go to lunch.

Everyone scrambles to exit.

Shore Patrol MP's escort Fungitis out of courtroom. Tears
well in his eyes. He struggles. As Judge and Officers file
out of the room he angrily screams,

                         FUNGITIS
              I did it for the defense of my
              nation. May my words echo in
              infamy to mock your injustice.

EXT. HEAVENLY HILLS - DAY

MARGARET and CORINNE drive on Barricade Lane. PENELOPE in
back seat, reads a sexy novel, "Midnight at Grannies Chateau."

They pull into driveway, screech to a stop, see cop cars.
COPS remove items from Margaret's house.

JENNIFER hysterically tails cops as they carry furniture into
moving van. Margaret backs out to street, drives away. COP
sees Margaret, jumps in patrol car, siren sings, chase is on.

INT. MARGARET'S CAR - DAY

MARGARET and CORINNE race fast, dodge cars and pedestrians
through winding Beverly Hills streets.

                         CORINNE
              What the heck is going on?

                         MARGARET
                    Goodman knows who I am.

MAN almost gets run over. His dog leaps on hood. Margaret
activates windshield washer. Dog leaps off.

                         CORINNE
                    How did he find out? And why are
                    they taking your things? They
                    need a court order to do that.
                    Don't they?

Margaret's head-on with a tour bus. Bus horn blows. Cop car
closes fast.

                         MARGARET
                    That little ratface Samuel
                    Goblingab. That's who. He's been
                    following us everywhere we go.
                    Goodman's using the drug
                    forfeiture law.

Miss bus by inches. Cop now on Margaret's tail.

                         CORINNE
                    They can't do that in Heavenly
                    Hills.
                         (frowning)
                    You don't sell drugs, do you?
                    Ohhh! Maybe when you served the
                    girls the fruit punch laced with
                    cellulose fiber. That's a
                    sedative, isn't it? Tranquilizes
                    the bowels.

Margaret blows HORN, passes cars like a maniac. Penelope
totally absorbed in the novel.

                         MARGARET
                    If they arrest Jennifer or harm
                    Fluffy, it'll be World War three.

COPS line street ahead with green trash cans. Margaret plows
through them.

Margaret crashes through security gate to a home.

                         CORINNE
                    Where are you going?

                         MARGARET
                    Just a little shortcut I know of.

They drive into back yard, hit diving board, sail over
swimming pool and straight down a brush covered hillside to
a road below. Cop car dives into pool.

EXT. LONG BEACH NAVAL YARD - DAY, BREAK OF DAWN

SAILOR plays Taps. FUNGITIS, blindfolded. MP's escort him
past SAILORS with rifles by their side. They walk him a ways
then stop.

OFFICER approaches, motions Fungitis to smoke a cigarette.
Fungitis declines. Officer blindfolds him, steps away.

Soft roll of drums. Fungitis breathes heavily, lips quiver.
Rifles load CLICK! CLICK! BLAM!

Fungitis's head jerks, BLAM! Jerks again. His head falls
limp, drops to chin. Exhales a burst of air.

Sound of FOOTSTEPS. Hand removes Fungitis's blindfold.

Fungitis snivels like a baby, tears well from bloodshot eyes
pour down his cheeks.

WIDER VIEW

SAILORS with rifles salute as Fungitis walks a gangplank to
a battleship.

Gangplank entrance displays a large arched banner, "Welcome
To USS Battleship Liberty. A Living History Museum. Admission
$3.75. Photograph With The Captain $8.95"

INT. DESERT BASE / COMMAND ROOM - DAY

MARGARET, CORINNE and PENELOPE. Margaret explains layout of
L.A. County jail on electronic map.

                    MARGARET
          You got it?

The girls nod and salute simultaneously.

                    MARGARET
                 (continuing)
          Okay, let's go!

They exit, see two TANKS leave the portal. GRANNIES in full
combat gear ride on top APC's.

GRANNIES follow, turn and salute. They proudly return and
hold salute.

STRAGGLER tries to catch up.

                    STRAGGLER
          I forgot to pack my Meta-
          Fibercill. I can't see without it!

INT. SUBMERGED SUBMARINE - DAY

Laundry items hang everywhere. Grannies wear fuzzy slippers,
bathrobes, rollers in hair.

SOAP OPERA on computer monitor - FRANK by an idle slot
machine, stares at it with his comatose expression. He's
dressed in white Al Capone attire. JEANETTE and SUSAN argue
over whom will keep Frank's winnings.

Monitor fades, Margaret's image appears.

                    MARGARET (V.O.)
               Rise and shine my little torpedoes.

Everyone stands to attention.

                    MARGARET (V.O.)
                    (continuing)
               Where's Bertha?

THERESA (80) approaches monitor.

                    THERESA
               She's in the engine room with
               Lanky fixing pipes.

Theresa yells into a brass tube,

                    THERESA
                    (continuing)
               Captain to the bridge.

BERTHA pops her head out of a floor plate. The plates lower
and she comes up the hatch stairwell.

                    MARGARET (V.O.)
                    (to Bertha)
               I'm downloading the plans to your
               computer. An inferno of a mission
               and we're relying on you to be on
               time. If you fail, we all fail.
                    (beat)
               The mission must succeed at all
               costs. Even if you must die!

Bertha recoils, frowns with shock.

Monitor screen goes dark. Message appears, "Downloading.
Wait state please. Download completed. Ready for print out.
Printer on?"

Bertha taps "Y" on keyboard, printer starts. LANKY pokes head
out of hatch. A bra dangles from his head.

Bertha reads printed message, "Rescue MEBOMS. L.A. County Jail. Use plan S-T-I-C-K-Y." A map prints.

EXT. BY L.A. COUNTY JAIL - DAY

FIVE GRANNIES disguised as PRISON GUARDS walk to work with small suitcases in hand. KAREN and PATTY (75) with them. MARGARET drives by, nods.

INT. JAIL - DAY

Shift change. Jail infested with GUARDS. GRANNIES flash ID cards, walk through control sallyport. Door slams shut on PATTY.

> CONTROL OFFICER
> I don't recognize you. Let me see
> your ID. card.

Patty hands over her ID, plays it cool. The other grannies nervously sweat bullets. Control room COP appears baffled, examines ID card and Patty.

> CONTROL COP
> This doesn't look like you.
> Please stand under the light so I
> can get a better look.

Patty glances to the other girls who nervously nod as though saying, "Do what he say's."

> PATTY
> I'm not moving another inch. I've
> had as much as I can take of this
> sexual harassment. I'm going to
> the Watch Commander and I'm filing
> on you!

Fear leaps from control officer's face.

> PATTY
> (continuing)
> How dare you say you want to get
> a better look at me! You're
> cornering me and you know it's
> against the rules.

Control cop stiffens, panics.

> CONTROL COP
> (stuttering)
> No, wait. I didn't mean it that
> way. I'm married, I got kids to
> feed. I can't lose my --

                         PATTY
               Open the door and I'll forget it
               happened.

Control cop hastily hands her the ID card, sallyport door
snaps open.

INT. DOWN THE HALL - DAY

GUARDS escort JENNIFER into Cell #219, upper tier. She holds
a cage. FLUFFY inside cage, growls.

PRISON GUARD affectionately inserts finger into cage OW!

INMATES laugh, guard sucks his thumb. Guard angrily whacks
cage with night stick. Fluffy hisses, ears pinned back,
swipes paw, rips his pants. Jennifer smiles.

SERIES OF SHOTS

EXT. JAIL EXERCISE YARD - DAY

- - YOUNG FEMALE inmates CHEER, stand in a circle. In the
center, GRANNY INMATE bench presses 200 pounds.

- - BUZZING noise overhead, a model airplane. GUARDS shoot at
it. Male and female INMATES fall to the ground. Bullet hits
wing, keeps flying, irritates guards as it buzzes by.
Inmates stand, resume lifting weights. CAPTIVE GRANNIES peer
out iron bar laced window.

- - PENELOPE on a nearby building roof operates controls of
airplane. She presses a button, plane takes a picture.
Picture of the inmate's swimming pool on a portable TV screen
by her side.

- - FEMALE inmates sun by the pool wear scant bikinis
imprinted with the words, "Property of L.A. County Jail."
The imprints precisely in the right places. Bikinis prison
issue gray & white stripe.

- - MALE INMATES wear same fashion tight swim gear circle
like sharks, make dates by REFRESHMENT STAND. The guy's buy
the GIRLS drinks. A sign, "Non-alcoholic beer and wine."

- - MALE GUARD stands by FEMALE INMATES giving him a back
massage, run their fingers through his hair. He tries to
kiss one, she backs away, rubs her index fingers as if he
were a naughty boy.

EXT. OSCAR'S HOT DOG STAND - DAY

SARAH with BULLDOG sees SAMUEL on sidewalk with hot dog in
hand. She unleashes the dog.

                          SARAH
                 Git'em, Petunia.

Dog scampers across the street, dodges traffic, causes a
fender-bender accident SCREECH! CLUNK!

Dog yaps annoyingly at Samuel. Irate drivers blast car
horns, yell. Samuel refuses to give the dog any food, kicks
at the pest, spills his coffee. Dog persists.

Samuel looks at Sarah across the street, dog lifts leg, pees
on Samuel's shoe. Samuel kicks again, loses his balance,
unconsciously lowers hand.

Dog leaps, snatches hot dog, runs over hoods of stopped cars.
Dog's tail wags. Sarah removes hot dog from dog's teeth,
smiles.

                          SARAH
                       (continuing)
                 Good girl! Good doggie!

Sarah gives half to her loyal friend. She eats the other
half.

                          SAMUEL
                 Leave me alone. I'll call the
                 cops.

                          SARAH
                 I'm watching you, Goblingab. And
                 I've got the battery acid right
                 here in my purse.

She pulls out a jar of sulfuric acid, smiles. Samuel
sheepishly walks away, looks over shoulder as he goes.

INT. MAYOR'S OFFICE - DAY

GOODMAN repeatedly slams fists on desk. SNITCH tap-dances on
desk, feet avoids fist blows.

                          GOODMAN
                 Those darned grannies. It's true.
                 It's true. It's the end of our
                 world.

                          SNITCH
                 What are you howling about?

                          GOODMAN
                 Mizrabella. She told me it would
                 happen. I went to see her --

GOODMAN'S DREAM

INT. MIZRABELLA'S HOUSE - DAY

GOODMAN intently gazes to CRYSTAL BALL, glows dimly.
MIZRABELLA (120) dressed as a Gypsy. Lights low. She peers
deeply into the ball.

                    MIZRABELLA
               I see dark days and bright nights.
               Wrinkled faces closing in for the
               kill.

                    GOODMAN
               What does it mean?

                    MIZRABELLA
               I don't know. I don't have my
               glasses on.

She puts on glasses, clears her throat.

                    MIZRABELLA
                    (continuing)
               The ball is fading. Put in more
               money!

Goodman inserts $100 bill into base of ball, it brightens,
projects a brief "Thank You" image.

Mizrabella concentrates deeply into the ball. She appears
crazed at what she sees.

                    GOODMAN
               What do you see?

INT. CRYSTAL BALL - NIGHT

MALE STRIPPERS dancing.

BACK TO SCENE

                    MIZRABELLA
               Darn it. I have the wrong
               channel. I need to get this ball
               fixed. It's acting weird. Okay,
               here we go. I see dark days and
               bright nights.

                    GOODMAN
               You already said that.

>   MIZRABELLA
>   That's what I see. You want me to
>   lie to you?
>   (looks into ball)
>   I see geezers tailing you.
>   Perhaps, a fan club? No, wait.
>   Gaze into the ball.

Goodman leans close to ball, eyes wide.

INT. CRYSTAL BALL - DAY

Slow motion image of GRANNIES with canes chase GOODMAN. His
clothes tattered, runs to a jail cell.

GUARD stands by the cell slowly waves his arm to hurry. Cell
door closing. A GRANNY'S hand close to his neck.

Crystal ball image dissolves.

>   MIZRABELLA
>   I'm afraid the ball has given up
>   the ghost.

END OF DREAM

INT. MAYOR'S OFFICE - DAY

>   SNITCH
>   You don't believe that hog wash,
>   do you?

GOODMAN curled in fetal position on floor, sucks his thumb.
SNITCH still stands on desk.

>   GOODMAN
>   Where's my biker gangs?

>   SNITCH
>   They went to Majestic Mountain to
>   raise money for the Spike
>   Foundation and to see if they can
>   kidnap some grannies.

>   GOODMAN
>   Good. Good. We must imprison
>   every living granny. All of them.
>   It's not safe with them roaming
>   about the streets.

Intercom light glows on "Listen Mode."

EXT. MAJESTIC MOUNTAIN THEME PARK - DAY

SPIKE, MAD DOG, BIG DADDY park Harley's near entrance. Mad
Dog wears a black Easy Rider hat. Pass metal detector, forced
to deposit guns in gun locker.

ROSEMARY (72) in employer uniform, holds a twisted snake
cane, gives receipt for guns.

Bikers buy tickets, pass through turnstile, purchase cotton
candy.

Rosemary's approached by LOLITA dressed in a security guard
uniform. Rosemary hands her the guns. Lolita stuffs them in
pocketbook, enters theme park.

Lolita opens a gate. Moving van enters loading area.
GRANNIES exit truck dressed in full battle gear. Rosemary
arrives, hands them the biker's guns.

INT. OBSERVATION TOWER / THEME PARK - DAY

MARGARET peers into coin operated viewer, sees the BIKERS,
speaks into two-way radio.

                    MARGARET
          Okay girls, here they come.

SERIES OF SHOTS

ATTACK SEQUENCE / VARIOUS LOCATIONS

EXT. MAJESTIC MOUNTAIN - DAY

- - CORINNE, PENELOPE and four GRANNIES in full battle gear,
ride the carrousel horses, blend in with children. Each
wears a small headset to communicate.

- - They leap off carrousel, follow BIKERS to "Japanese
Garden." Bikers notice, run. Grannies open fire tearing
garden to smithereens. PEOPLE meditate in lotus positions in
a state of bliss and contentment.

- - BIKERS jump a fence, hop onto "Log Jam Ride." GRANNIES
wait for the next log to arrive, then all leap in
simultaneously. They pop rounds at the bikers whenever they
get a clear shot.

- - At the top of the hill just before the last slide, BIKERS
see a GRANNY in a Majestic Mountain uniform at the controls.
She smiles, yanks a big lever, log accelerates. Bikers
panic, jump out, tumble down a grass hill.

- - GRANNIES scream as they ride the log down the big hill, hold rifles sky high. They splash into the station, confused, see the empty log ahead of them. KIDS stare at the grannies in awe.

- - MARGARET in observation tower sees the bikers.

                MARGARET
        They're in the Petting Zoo. Move
        in!

EXT. PETTING ZOO / THEME PARK - DAY

BIKERS try to blend into the CROWD of kids petting lambs. GRANNIES barge in, open fire. Rams slam horns into bikers butts OUCH!

KIDS and PARENTS in petting zoo cheer for the grannies, ask for autographs. GRANNIES oblige.

EXT. CAGED AREA / THEME PARK - DAY

BIKERS turn a corner, climb a solid fence, They sit, out of breath, cough, frantically smoke cigarettes, hold chests in pain.

                SPIKE
        We're safe here.

                BIG DADDY
        Keep quiet!

Big Daddy's panicky, scared.

                MAD DOG
            (whispering)
        Shhh! The grannies are on the
        other side.

GRUNTING sound o.s.

                SPIKE
        What's that?

                MAD DOG
        Shhh!

BABOON leaps on a rock, grunts loudly, heads turn fast. Disturbed beast flashes teeth, eyebrows fluctuate up and down.

                SPIKE
        Is it pissed off?

Big Daddy's eyebrows mimic baboon.

                         BIG DADDY
                    I think it is.

Baboon charges, leaps on Spike's back. It's doing a real
number on him. Fists whack his head and back at incredible
speed. Mad Dog and Big Daddy gag Spike so he can't scream.

Spike's eyes big as moons. Baboon jumps off, points to a
fence. Bikers eagerly hop it. Baboon hurls a rock, hits Mad
Dog in butt.

INT. OBSERVATION TOWER / THEME PARK - AFTERNOON

MARGARET's eyes search, speaks into radio.

                         MARGARET
                    Fan out. We lost them.

EXT. THEME PARK / BY CARNIVAL GAMES - DAY

GRANNIES fan out, but still remain as a group. They see a
BIKER with back turned, open fire TAT! TAT! TAT! Biker
crumbles into slivers, shatters like glass. A glass statue
of Brando.

EXT. A FENCED AREA / THEME PARK - DAY

Mountainous area. BIKERS sneak along rocks, splash through
waterfalls.

                         SPIKE
                    Hey guys look over here, a cave.

Near cave entrance, MAD DOG picks up black stones that
crumble if squeezed. Slips them to pockets.

                         BIG DADDY
                      Might be a good place to hold up
                      awhile.

INT. CAVE / THEME PARK - DAY

SPIKE'S cigarette lighter casts eerie shadows. MAD DOG
follows last. A prolonged BURP o.s. Mad Dog urges them to
go on. They come upon a large open chamber full of bones.

Looking up, see a MOUNTAIN LION on a ledge. Lion rises, leaps
at them with a bloodcurdling roar. They run out, scale a
fence.

Lion rips BIG DADDY'S leather pants wide open with one swipe.
He wears pink panties.

EXT. FENCED AREA / FLOWER GARDEN / THEME PARK - DAY

BIKERS in a delightfully refreshing flower garden stand in
awe when they see a sign, "The Garden Of Eden."

They explore the place and come upon another sign on a post
embedded in the soil placed by beautiful flowering plants.
Sign reads, "Alligator Ducks."

SPECTATORS with worried expressions of anticipation stand on
a platform behind a fence. Bikers hold hands to gain
assurances.

MUSIC plays. Lights dim. A clap of THUNDER, lightning
flashes.

                    COMMANDING VOICE (V.O.)
               Yea shall have dominion over all
               creatures of the earth. Except
               the ducks!

Flowerbed comes alive as if a breeze gently rustles stems.

DUCKS waddle out of the flower bed, tear into the bikers
leather boots and pants, rip away huge chunks.

Spectators SCREAM with the bikers. These ducks draw blood as
they clamp their beaks onto the bikers skin. Duck latches
onto Big Daddy's rear, won't let go.

Barbed wire laces the other three fences. Signs on each
fence, "Polar Bear", "Rattlesnakes", "Fire Ants."

They run to a apple tree with hangman's noose on it. Ducks
quack and bite as they climb trunk to a branch, then it
snaps. Branch crashes on a barbed wire fence.

They tumble into,

EXT. FIRE ANT PIT / THEME PARK - AFTERNOON

BIKERS escape a brief encounter with FIRE ANTS breathing real
fire. Clothes totally in shards from the duck attack, and
now burnt from fire ants, they shimmy over a small concrete
wall, drop to freedom on other side.

Duck growls, still clamped firmly on BIG DADDY'S rear. SPIKE
sweet-talks and pets the duck. Duck lets go, flies away
quacking with a piece of underwear in beak.

INT. OBSERVATION TOWER / THEME PARK - SUNSET

MARGARET sees the BIKERS, radios the grannies.

                    MARGARET
               They are heading to coaster.

EXT. SKI LIFT RIDE / THEME PARK - SUNSET

GRANNIES descend into the station. As they dismount,
CORINNE'S belt catches on the bucket's gate. The ride can't
stop so up she goes dangling from the swinging gate. She's
screaming her head off.

Gate hinge breaks. Corinne free-falls. Grannies catch her
and away they go.

EXT. ROLLER COASTER / THEME PARK - SUNSET

BIKERS see a long line waiting to ride a wood duel track
rollercoaster. They hesitate.

MALE ATTENDANT (18) stands on the right side of the train
station by an empty roller coaster. He waves his hand,
invites bikers to board train.

                    SPIKE
          They're opening a new line. Let's
          go.

Bikers run as fast as they can through the empty maze of
zigzag crowd control railings.

They hop into the train's front seat. Attendant wastes no
time locking them in.

As they sit, they notice nobody budges to board train. PEOPLE
in the other long line stare with wide eyes.

                    BIG DADDY
               (to attendant)
          How come nobody's boarding?

Attendant smiles deviously, points to sign, "Warning! This
train runs backwards. Ride at your own risk!"

Bikers scream like little girls as the coaster rumbles slowly
out of the station, in reverse.

Around they go, pass the first curve, heading to chain lift.
Up they go, CLICKITY, CLACK, CLACK.

At the top of the hill there's a booth for an attendant to
safety check train before it disengages the chain lift.
ROSEMARY sits in the booth. Bikers scream in horror when
they see her.

She gives them a twisted smile as she lashes out to hit them
with her cane. Down they go descending hill #1, backwards.

- - We can see from the forward running car all the empty
cars and the BIKERS in the last car.

                              SPIKE
                    Oh, no. Look!

- - As they rise hill #2, they catch a glimpse of LOLITA.
Her hatchet, chops a wood support beam at ground level.

  - - BIKERS approach train station, MALE ATTENDANT stands
under an electric sign flashing red, "Apply Brakes Now."
Warning buzzer and red light pulsates.

He's totally occupied, kisses a foxy BRUNETTE in scant
clothing.

- - BIKERS train rumbles into station, exceeds safe design
speed, screeching, grinding steel, fan shaped showers of gold
sparks spray from wheels.

BIKER'S scream, round the curve, link to chain lift.

- - Three quarters up the big hill, BIKERS see forward
running train on parallel track climb the big hill. It's the
GRANNIES, they shoot. CORINNE in front seat.

- - ROSEMARY pokes cane from booth doorway, releases safety
handlebar lock on bikers train. Handlebar flips up. BIKERS
scream in horror.

BIKERS rise, stand, desperately grasp vertical handlebar.

Bikers yanked by centrifugal force right out of their seats
upside-down. Train descends big hill.

- - Up and down hills and curves BIKERS flip in and out of
the car holding on for dear life. They see LOLITA, with a
chain saw cutting support beams.

                          BIG DADDY
                    Spike, give me your rosary beads.
                    I left them on my bike.

Spike fondles beads, prays fast.

                            SPIKE
                    Get your own.

Big Daddy snatches them away.

- - GRANNIES in forward running train shoot as best they can.
Two stand on running boards fire pistols. Wood chips and
sparks fly, light bulbs burst throughout chase.

- - BIKERS see LOLITA. She rips a wood support beam away
with bare hands, tosses it over shoulder.

                          MAD DOG
                    I don't want to die.

MAD DOG hugs BIG DADDY. He shoves Mad Dog away.

- - Each time the coasters briefly pass each other BIKERS
duck low. MAD DOG lobs black rocks at the GRANNIES - SPLAT!

- - GRANNIES ride a straight section of track near MYSTIC
LAKE shooting at the BIKERS' train wheels.

- - LOLITA stands in the middle of the biker's track,
crowbars track rails.

- - Both steel rails bent upward at 30 degree angle. BIKERS
train takes the curve, enters straight section of track
heading right for LOLITA.

- - BIKERS stand, scream. LOLITA'S shoe stuck in track. At
the very last moment, she leaps to safety, leaves shoe behind.

- - Coaster slams the ramp, leaps into air backwards. Entire
coaster flies mid-air horizontally over a lake.

BIKERS POV - COLOSSUS moves away as a space ship leaves earth.

Expressions of sheer horror. MAD DOG'S hat flips off.

- - BIKERS coaster loses momentum, snakes violently. Far-end
car flips upside-down. Then, the next, like dominoes. Bikers
flip too.

They stand upside-down. Coaster shakes the bikers out like
a salt/pepper shaker.

Down they go, splash into MYSTIC LAKE. Coaster crumples into
shallow water a few feet away. Bikers swim.

INT. SHACK / MYSTIC LAKE RAFT / THEME PARK - NIGHT

Raft with a crude shack on it. BIKERS climb on, enter the
shack.

                    SPIKE
          I say we stay put. Those grannies
          will think we drowned.

They peer out window, see GRANNIES search shoreline with
flashlights by the mangled coaster. One of them picks up Mad
Dog's hat floating on the water.

INT. OBSERVATION TOWER / THEME PARK - NIGHT

MARGARET descends glass window elevator, observes Majestic
Mountain glittering in the night below.

BACK TO SCENE

BIKERS sit on edge of raft, splash their feet in the dark water like little girls.   They see a CROWD of people fill grandstands.

Relaxing MUSIC commences from PA system.

              MAD DOG
      What's this?

              SPIKE
      Motorboat stunt show. I remember
      seeing the TV commercial.

              MAD DOG
      At night?

Grandstand lights grow dim. MUSIC fades.

            ANNOUNCEMENT (V.O.)
      Ladies and gentlemen. Welcome to
      Mystic Lake. Mr. Wizard, are you
      ready?

            THE WIZARD (V.O.)
      I was just taking a nap. Excuse
      me. My, my, my, we have a
      wonderful audience tonight. I've
      been working on a brand new spell.
      Would you like to see it?

Crowd CHEERS. Fast tempo MUSIC begins.

BIKER'S POV

Entire lake erupts into a torrent of white magnesium fire and sparks. Rockets scream every which way imaginable.

Two Fountains overhead explode BOOM! Millions of gold & white sparks pour onto the raft, a fusillade of firecrackers pop and dance on deck.

Bikers dive into water. They swim, dodge angry rockets and exploding fireworks.

At shoreline, AUDIENCE applauds. Bikers play along, bow, as they skip away.

EXT. GRANDSTAND / THEME PARK - NIGHT

CORINNE and PENELOPE in audience see the BIKERS. Penelope fires eighteen 9mm rounds from her pistol so fast the muzzle flashes appear as one continuous flame.

Bikers slide around a corner in the nick of time. Corinne
shouts into her headset,

                    CORINNE
          Positive I.D. on bikers. Mystic
          Lake. Heading to exit. Pronto!

EXT. MAJESTIC MOUNTAIN / THEME PARK ENTRANCE - NIGHT

California Highway patrol car parked next to biker's
motorcycles. CHP OFFICER directs traffic nearby. His back to
us, he's busy, takes phone numbers from GIRLS in convertibles.

Two CHP OFFICERS slip into front seat of patrol car. We
don't see their faces. BIKERS mount and start their bikes.
MARGARET stands in front of them.

She holds a little bell in her hand.

                    MARGARET
          Stop, or I'll ring the bell. I
          mean it.

Bikers laugh. She rings the bell. GRANNIES surround them
with weapons drawn.

Bikers surrender. MAD DOG slyly reaches for a gun under the
seat. CORINNE, points her long barrel semi-auto 357 magnum.

                    CORINNE
          I dare you.

They handcuff the sniveling bikers, force them into back seat
of CHP patrol car.

Margaret approaches with bell in hand.

                    BIG DADDY
          You got nothing on us. Well be
          out in two hours. Then I'll deal
          with you on my terms.

Margaret rings her bell again.

                    MARGARET
                 (to officers in front
                  seat)
          Take 'em away.

CHP vehicle leaves.

Bikers look out rear window. Patrol car rolls past CHP
officer directing traffic. GRANNIES kick motorcycles to
pavement.

CHP officer runs to car, waves hands, yells, loses ground,
slows to a stop. Takes off his hat, throws it to the ground,
kicks it sky-high.

                    BIG DADDY
                (to cops in front
                  seat)
        They can't do that. It's illegal.

Two COPS in front seat slowly face the bikers. They're
GRANNIES! Chins drop, they scream in horror.

INT. OUR LADY OF VICTORY CHURCH / EAST L.A. - NIGHT

LATINO GRANNIES play bingo in a hall filled with cigarette
smoke so thick it reminds us of smog. A GRANNY speaks into
microphone.

                    ANNOUNCER (V.O.)
            We are interrupting the game for
            an important news development.

Back stage curtain draws open, large screen TV rolled
forward. Lights dim.

ON TV

                    ANCHORMAN TOM BROKER (V.O.)
            A paramilitary group known as
            "Mebom" battles police and gangs
            in the San Fernando valley. Our
            live action footage is awesome and
            may be too bitchin' for most
            viewers. Christine,

TV inserts CHRISTINE (30) reporter at the scene. White and
red tracer rounds bounce off buildings and sidewalks in b.g.
Noise of gunfire intense.

CORINNE crouches low, fires a bazooka, blows up a parked
police car. PENELOPE fires grenade launcher.

Two COPS exit fireball engulfed in flames, act as nothing
were wrong, talk about how thirsty they are.

The human torches enter "Harry's Dunking Dognuts" coffee
shop. PATRONS dash out, scream in panic.

                    CHRISTINE (V.O.)
            I'm here on Tobias avenue.
            Intense fighting rages in Panorama
            City. Meboms advance at a
            feverish pace.

Bradley clanks down street, turret sprays machine gun fire, shatters home windows. Latino GANGSTERS run through alleys between homes, throw Molotov cocktails.

Rear hatch opens, screaming GRANNY GI's charge out shooting. Gangsters fall like leaves. They surrender. M2 rolls on down the street. TELEVISION NEWS TEAM follows M2.

> CHRISTINE (V.O.)
> (continuing)
> Rumors of grannies conspiring to take back the streets is evidently true. Mebom is no fantasy. They are a well trained army with devastating firepower. They are winning!

WIDER VIEW

Latino GRANNIES cheer.

> LATINO GRANNIES
> Go Mebom! Go, go, Mebom!

ON TV

> TOM BROKER (V.O.)
> We have word another battle's raging by Lost Angus, City Hall. Lets go to our reporter at the scene. Clifford,

CLIFFORD (40) reporter on scene.

> CLIFFORD (V.O.)
> Yes, Tom, we're at the Federal Courthouse building.

A mass of 15-rockets stream tight red flames whizzes perilously over Clifford's head. He ducks, interrupts his reporting. Rockets slam through the wall of the COURTHOUSE building. Nothing happens.

Clifford rises, and just when he does, the entire south face of the building explodes outward in a multicolored ball of magnesium stars. Clifford dives to pavement.

TV picture jumpy as camera crew run for cover.

Police HELICOPTER shines candlepower, lights up the area just ahead. Camera crew focuses on it.

A GRANNY launches stinger missile. It snakes upward barely misses helicopter, explodes, bursts into whizzing mini-rockets like a hive of bees.

INT. HELICOPTER - NIGHT

                    COPILOT (V.O.)
                  (to pilot)
              Throttle up. This ain't no street
              riot, it's a war.

PILOTS see GRANNIES in searchlight beam shoot it out with
POLICE. COPS, SPINY and his GANG behind cop car fire
shotguns.

M1A1 Abrams tank turns corner, advances to them. They run
BOOM! Cop car disintegrates to itsy-bitsy white hot sizzling
shrapnel. Sparking fragments spin and buzz on the ground
like toy tops.

Helicopter soars over high-rise building. MARGARET in a blue
uniform stands on a ledge, speaks MOS in radio.

Bullets spray the edge of the building. Margaret falls over
ledge, opens parachute before she hits bottom. She runs.
COPS follow. Typical shoot-out.

Margaret throws huge "Granny Apple" firecrackers as hand
grenades, keeps cops at bay. BOOM! BOOM!

Jeep comes to her rescue. Margaret hops in, hurls Granny
Apples as they zig-zag away. KABOOM!

Cop cars close in. Margaret works the machine gun. Cop cars
roll over.

INT. OUR LADY OF VICTORY CHURCH - NIGHT

Latino GRANNIES rise to their feet and cheer.

                    LATINO GRANNIES
                  (randomly)
              "Get'em, Homes!" "Give'em a taste
              of granny power!" "Go, go,
              homegirls!"

ON TV

Helicopter veers out of harms way. CLIFFORD stands. TANK
stops in street WHAM! A 30 foot orange flame lights up the
area from muzzle blast.

TV picture shakes. Red tracer travels a mile up the street.
Then, an orange ball of flame bursts in the distance.
Seconds later, a muffled BOOM!

Two BRADLEY ME2's race by, head toward the explosion. Platoon
of GRANNY GI's trudge wearily behind it.

Clifford sees MARGARET in the jeep. Distant gunfire erupts down the street. Tracers fill b.g.

> CLIFFORD (V.O.)
> Tell us your objective?

> MARGARET (V.O.)
> No more corruption. No more
> gangs. No more crime.

Margaret looks straight into camera.

> MARGARET (V.O.)
> (continuing)
> Our grandchildren deserve a better
> life. Yours too! Don't just sit
> their scrutinizing the TV. Get
> out of your rocking chairs and
> take back your street. I give you
> the authority.

Another TANK plows up the street at full speed. GRANNIES heads pop out of hatches.

> GRANNIES
> (randomly)
> L.A. is taken." "East L.A. here
> we come!"

Margaret gives a thumbs-up, platoon advances, reload rifles as they march forward behind jeep. CORINNE hops to the machine gun, lays down cover fire. PENELOPE joins, sweeps grenade launcher, looks mean.

INT. ROOF OF CITY HALL - NIGHT

GOODMAN, SNITCH and SAMUEL stare at MARGARET and GRANNIES as they load shell into Howitzer BOOM!

Top of City Hall blasted to pieces.

INT. OUR LADY OF VICTORY CHURCH - NIGHT

LATINO GRANNIES change clothes, reveal faded tattoos on their bodies from the days they were once young homegirls. One looks right at us.

> LATINO GRANNY
> Once a homegirl, always a homegirl.

> ANOTHER GRANNY
> This time homegirls gonna kick
> homeboys butts!

EXT. SIDEWALK / EAST L.A. - NIGHT

LATINO GRANNIES dressed in baggy pants, wear rim hats just
like the male gang members wear.

They see SPINY and his HOMEBOYS on a street corner. They
sell firecrackers, throw burritos at cars.

Grannies with canes silently approach, roll up sleeves. Spiny
believes he sees a rival gang.

Homeboys block sidewalk ready for a confrontation. They pull
out guns as grannies approach.

Spiny can't believe his eyes, face distorts.

                    SPINY
          Grandma?

LITTLE HEART and homeboys see their grandmothers. Grannies
whip canes, simultaneously flick the guns from homeboys hands
WHACK! Right on the wrists OUCH!

Grannies reach out, pinch their ears, drag them away.
Homeboys sing the Ow! Ow! song.

                    GRANNIES
                (randomly)
          "You think you can outsmart this
          homegirl do you?" "Enough of this
          nonsense.

          Get in the house, right now."
          "I'll show you who's going to run
          these streets."

They pull, yank, drag homeboys by the ear down the street.
Homeboys plead promises and resolutions, but the grannies
won't let go of those ears. Little Heart resists, but his
GRANNY has an ironclad grip.

They enter homes. Street cleared. OLD LATINO MEN fearfully
stare out the windows.

TANKS and M2's clank around a corner, crawl slowly down the
street. Gun turrets turn left and right.

Latino grannies rush out of their homes into the street to
greet the GRANNY GI's. Tanks and M2's stop. They hug each
other celebrating in the street.

Some grannies bring tacos and salted Margaritas. Supply
truck arrives towing a howitzer.

MARGARET exits truck, joins the celebration. CORINNE and
PENELOPE arrive in jeep.

Margaret looks right at us. She's tired and dirty. Uniform torn to shreds.

> MARGARET
> Don't mess with granny!

She hugs the grannies, departs in a military helicopter.

EXT. PACIFIC OCEAN - DAY

Object falls from military helicopter, splashes into water.

INT. UNDER THE WATER - DAY

The object - Diving bell unites to pink submarine.

EXT, / INT. SEWER TUNNEL - DAY

Submarine dives, enters a submerged tunnel. A little ways inside, tunnel half-filled with water. Sub rises to the surface travels toward us.

As it passes, diesel engines roar. Sub makes a sharp 45-degree turn, vanishes from view.

INT. FURTHER UP THE TUNNEL - DAY

ROGER (21) and TOM (65) in a small dingy motoring along. They scan a map.

They wear uniforms. Back of shirts reads, "Lost Angus Sewer Dept. Nothing defiles us, nothing!"

> ROGER
> Tom, you certain we're heading the
> right way?

Tom sniffs the air.

> TOM
> I can tell by the smell we're
> close.

Submarine approaches dingy at high speed. Roger and Tom turn as they hear the roar of the sub's diesel engines bear down on them like a locomotive highballing at maximum throttle.

> ROGER
> Look out!

> TOM
> What the? Full throttle. It's a
> whale!

The little boat churns a pitiful plume of bubbles as the tiny prop struggles to move the dingy forward. Submarine looms dangerously close.

>   TOM
>   (continuing)
>   Faster! Faster! Turn right into
>   tunnel "A"

"Y" intersection just ahead. Dingy can't turn into tube "A" as the current's too strong for the tiny outboard motor PUTT! PUTT! PUTT!

>   ROGER
>   I got it to the floor. It's the
>   best it can do.

Submarine right on top of them. Before it collides, sub abruptly stops. Sanitation workers stare at it. Sub backs up, accelerates into tube "A"

>   TOM
>   That does it. My wife is right.
>   It's time I retire.

Dingy floats downstream and fades into the darkness.

>   TOM (V.O.)
>   They say the gas will get you in
>   time. One guy seen a marching band.

INT. SUBMARINE - DAY

LANKY monitors sonar screen. GRANNIES fix their hair, apply make-up, prepare for a night on the town.

>   LANKY
>   We're almost there.

>   BERTHA
>   How much time we have left?

>   LANKY
>   Two minutes.

MARGARET exits diving bell, soaked in water. Everyone stands to attention.

>   MARGARET
>   Get this sub moving!

The crew jump to their stations.

```
INT. JAIL / CELL BLOCK - DAY

PRISON GUARD walks away from us along a tier, bangs black PR-
24 nightstick along cell bars.  A hand extended through the
bars of Cell #120 holds a mirror.

Guard's butt image on mirror.  Guard spins around, raps the
inmate's wrist with nightstick OUCH!  Other INMATES laugh.

Mirror falls, shatters into sparkling diamonds glittering on
the floor.

Prison Guard casually walks on as if nothing has happened,
then stops at Cell #117. Guard turns toward us, it's PATTY.

                    PATTY
                 (whispering)
          I can't get anymore ice cream.
          They locked the freezer.

GRANNIES and JENNIFER in the cell pout.

PATTY moves on, clangs night stick along the bars.

KAREN dressed as a prison guard comes toward us, a male
INMATE pushes a cart. Inmate lifts a bag from the cart.

                    KAREN
                 (to inmate)
          Those bags go to cell one-
          seventeen.

They approach Cell #117, deliver bags to DEBBIE, DONNA,
SAPPHIRE, JENNIFER, and other captive GRANNIES in the cell.
Eleven total.

Karen slips Debbie a large brass key.  They move on,
distribute romance books to male INMATES.

Distant moans o.s. from Cell #120. Two CONVICTS taunt.

                    FIRST CONVICT
          I thought you liked tough girls?

                    SECOND CONVICT
          She loves you, homes.

PATTY inserts her PR-24 into Cell #120, swings it wildly
trying to get another hit.

                    PATTY
          Come a little closer sweetheart so
          I can crack your skull.

                    INJURED INMATE
          Help!  Somebody call the cops!
```

MOMENTS LATER

GRANNIES exit Cell #117 in prison guard uniforms to,

EXT. JAIL / EXERCISE YARD - DAY

Escaping GRANNIES fan out, blend in with GUARDS supervising INMATES.

EXT. JAIL / SWIMMING POOL / EXERCISE YARD - DAY

Water boils. Concrete bottom cracks wide open, up comes the SUBMARINE.

Lounging inmates scatter, scream, "Earthquake!"

GUARD in gun tower fires his mini-14 rifle at the sub KAPOW! All the inmates tumble to the ground.

SERIES OF SHOTS

JAIL ATTACK SEQUENCE

- - GRANNIES rush out of sub, fire Gatling gun BURRP! Yard gun tower disintegrates into a mass of toothpicks. COP tumbles out, lands safely with his mini-parachute.

- - MARGARET shouts orders from conning tower. She shoots a flare gun at guard towers. Fires start.

- - MISSILE LAUNCH obliterates another tower with a huge explosion. GUARD in tower soars in mid-air. All that stands, four jagged smoldering foundation I-beams. Guard splashes in swimming pool by sub.

- - GUARDS along gunwalk fire on the sub. Gatling gun belches BURRP! Bullets shear the gunwalk supports, the entire platform crashes to the ground. Guards dangle from window sills.

- - GUARDS run along roof, stop and take aim. BURRP! Off they go, land in pile of grass clippings and trash containers.

- - GUARDS pour out of a doorway firing as they run. They see Gatling gun barrel rotate out of ammo.

- - Another missile launch, lands nose-down square into center of yard. Its fuse burns internally, emits blue smoke from a small hole POOF! Flag pops up, "REVENGE OF THE GRANNIES."

Missile explodes, flings yellow immobilizing slime on inmates and guards. A rubbery glue.

- - Disguised GRANNIES run to the sub. MARGARET shoots a tear gas shell.

- - JENNIFER, holds FLUFFY's cage, runs. She trips, Fluffy
tumbles out, lands all four feet onto a INMATE's rear OW!
He's stuck in the glue. Jennifer won't leave Fluffy.

- - MARGARET'S restrained by LANKY and BERTHA. More COPS
arrive on scene, get stuck in glue.

                    MARGARET
          Jennifer, run! We can't wait.

Jennifer's hands become entangled in glue.

- - Disguised GRANNIES leap on board, drop into hatches, down
sub goes. More Guards arrive, shoot rifles at sub as it
descends into sewer. Thuds of lead strike superstructure.

- - Jennifer and Fluffy captured, returned to jail.

INT. MAYOR'S OFFICE / CITY HALL - DAY

GOODMAN, SNITCH, SAMUEL in room. Samuel rubs plunger with
shoe polish. Goodman defiantly stares at him.

                    GOODMAN
          Escaped? A submarine in a
          swimming pool? You're out of your
          minds.

                    SNITCH
          I don't know where they are hiding
          Spiny, Spike, Mad Dog and Big
          Daddy. The gangs won't leave
          their homes. They're afraid.

                    SAMUEL
          I lost my camera and film. Can I
          borrow some money?

                    GOODMAN
          Get out. All of you. Out!

SNITCH and SAMUEL leave. They don't close the door. Enter
elevator.

MOMENTS LATER

A commotion of voices and footsteps. Goodman sees a small
army of GRANNY'S rush toward him from hallway.

He slams the door, locks it, flicks a small switch under his
desk.

EXT. MAYORS OFFICE / HALLWAY - DAY

PENELOPE aims grenade launcher to door. GRANNIES step back,
cover their ears.

BACK TO SCENE

Door implodes into room BOOM! GRANNIES rush in. GOODMAN
reaches for handgun in desk drawer. A boot slams drawer
closed on his hand OUCH!

He looks up, it's MARGARET, dressed in sparkling white
uniform.

                    MARGARET
          It's over, Mr. Goodman.

Goodman tightly holds his injured wrist, totally defeated.

                    GOODMAN
          Well, you must be Margaret. I
          wasn't expecting to meet you so
          soon.

                    MARGARET
          Life is full of surprises.

                    GOODMAN
          Before you take me in, may I
          please use the restroom? This has
          been quite a day.

Margaret waves CORINNE and PENELOPE to check out restroom.
They return.

                    CORINNE
          It's okay. We're ten stories up.

Margaret nods.

INT. HALLWAY - DAY

CORINNE and PENELOPE escort GOODMAN to restroom. He enters,
closes door, pokes head out.

                    GOODMAN
          No peeking.

Corinne and Penelope kick door, OUCH!

INT. RESTROOM - DAY

GOODMAN locks door, stands on toilet seat, pushes aside
acoustic ceiling tile, removes a green back pack. He straps
it on, flushes toilet, steps back, makes a running CRASH dive
head-first through window.

CORINNE and PENELOPE hear glass break. They rap on door. No
answer. Kick door in.

MARGARET dashes in, looks out window, sees GOODMAN float to
ground, land, run into ADAM'S RESTAURANT across the street.
His parachute drags behind him.

Cop cars arrive, screech to a halt below.

Margaret grabs her radio. Her hands shake.

                    MARGARET
            Adam's restaurant, hurry.

Her face raked with fear.

                    MARGARET
                (continuing; to
                 grannies)
            We're trapped!

They run to the elevator, desperately press call button.
Power disconnected.

INT. FIRE ESCAPE - DAY

GRANNIES race down fire escape stairs. Two flights down,
they see heavily armed COPS, guns drawn. Grannies fire.
PENELOPE out of ammo. They retreat.

Grannies scatter back upstairs. COPS descend stairs. Cops
shoot. Grannies shoot. They throw Granny Apple fruits
SPLAT! Retreat to,

INT. BY MAYOR'S OFFICE / HALLWAY - DAY

GRANNIES panic. Elevator bell DINGS, door slides open, COPS
exit. Simultaneously, COPS exit from fire escape.

Grannies surrounded. Reluctantly, they drop their weapons.
Cops reveal handcuffs.

                    MARGARET
                (to cops)
            Would you bound and gag your
            grandmother?

                    COP
            We don't trust anyone over sixty.
                (to cops)
            If they try anything, hog-tie them.

EXT. FRONT STEPS / CITY HALL - DAY

COPS escort MARGARET and the GRANNIES down the stairs.
PEDESTRIANS stare.

SAMUEL stands three steps down from the top. He sees his own
grandmother, CORINNE.

                         SAMUEL
               Grandma!

Corinne looks, but turns away. Grannies cross the street to,

INT. ADAM'S RESTAURANT - DAY

GOODMAN and SNITCH have JENNIFER hostage. Jennifer holds
FLUFFY.

MARGARET and her defeated group enter. COPS wait outside on
sidewalk.

                         GOODMAN
               Margaret, we meet again so soon?
               I'll give you Jennifer in exchange
               for my biker friends.

                         MARGARET
                    (politely)
               Then what? Back to business as
               usual?

Goodman gives Margaret a full-swing backhanded slap. She
staggers from the blow. She gets another, and another,
crumples to floor. Jennifer fumes.

                         JENNIFER
               Leave her alone!

Fluffy hisses.

Margaret tries to get up, Goodman kicks her hard in the ribs.
Margaret holds her chest, wheezes for air.

                         SNITCH
               She's having a heart attack!

Margaret's breathing slows. Her head falls gently on her
shoulder, side of her face touches floor. Her hands relax,
slide away.

Goodman shows no pity. He motions COPS outside to drag her
body out into the street of fast traffic.

                         JENNIFER
                    (explodes)
               You killed my mother!

EXT. STREET - DAY

SAMUEL approaches MARGARET'S still body. Cars swerve to
avoid the body. Samuel peers into restaurant window, sees
CORINNE sobbing. GOODMAN threateningly points his finger at
her nose.

Ambulance arrives.

TWO COPS on sidewalk open back door, remove stretcher from
ambulance. They place Margaret on it, pull a white sheet
over her head, slip her into ambulance.

PARAMEDICS remain in ambulance front seat. We don't see
their faces. Ambulance leaves without sirens.

Samuel, heartbroken, walks around a corner. As he turns the
corner he's face-to-face with a growling BULLDOG.

It's SARAH. In her rubber glove a bottle of sulfuric acid.
Sponge in other hand.

                    SARAH
          Samuel Goblingab. Take your pick.
          Hot ivory teeth or a sponge bath
          of acid.

Bulldog flashes teeth, barks, growls.

                    SAMUEL
          You're making a big mistake. I
          don't work for Goodman no more.
          I'm gonna rescue my grandmother,
          Corinne, and the others, right now.

                    SARAH
          You? Rescue? Ha! This I got to
          see. Let's go. Just remember, if
          you change your mind, I'll be
          right behind you. And I hope you
          fail.

Samuel moves on, Sarah follows. She has a leash tied to his
belt.

INT. AMBULANCE - DAY

PARAMEDICS turn around, look at MARGARET. They're GRANNIES.

                    TWO GRANNIES
                  (simultaneously)
          Rise and shine sweetpea.

Margaret sits up, holds her sore jaw, pants from holding her
breath. Paramedics hand her a radio.

                    MARGARET
          Okay girls, roll in and let 'em
          have it!

EXT. STREET / BY ADAM'S RESTAURANT - DAY

Two Abrams TANKS clank down the street. Cars peel out of its
way. The big guns open fire BOOM! BOOM! Two unoccupied cop
cars totally disintegrate. Splinters of hot smoking metal
sputter in the street.

A small section of car door smolders. Emblem reads, "Lost
Angus Police. To serve and to protect." Boot stomps on it.

COPS and PEDESTRIANS look to the sky, jaws sink, they run.

Granny SOLDIERS fall from sky in parachutes, they shoot at
cops. Under canopies the phrase, "MEBOM LOVES YOU."

Most land in street, some dangle helplessly on street lights,
window air conditioners, telephone poles, parking meters.

One GRANNY crashes through metal store front awning, knocks
over trash cans below.

ANOTHER lands in a commercial trash container.

ANOTHER lands on hood of passing cop car. She's points her
rifle at windshield, car stops.

INT. ADAM'S RESTAURANT - DAY

GOODMAN looks out the window, sees his world go up in smoke.
He hears o.s. the CLINK of tanks under the rapid fire of
turret machine guns.

COPS on foot retreat down the street.

BACK TO SCENE

Two APC's arrive, slam brakes, steel tracks rip asphalt.
Rear hatch lowers, army GRANNIES pour out, spray a fusillade
of bullets up and down the street.

Big guns on tanks fire again BOOM! BOOM! Two stores explode
near the restaurant.

Street cleared. Not a COP or PEDESTRIAN in sight. Tank
muzzles level to restaurant windows.

INT. ADAM'S RESTAURANT - DAY

GRANNIES in force storm inside restaurant's front and rear
doors simultaneously. Freeze right in their tracks. GOODMAN
has a 9mm PISTOL to JENNIFER's head.

                    GOODMAN
          Go ahead, shoot me.

Everyone backs off a little to take the pressure off Goodman.

Jennifer shivers with fright. FLUFFY too. She holds the cat close to her.

Goodman cocks hammer on gun CLICK!

>   GOODMAN
>   (continuing)
>   All of you, get out now or she's
>   going to heaven today.

Granny assault team backs off, clumsily bump into each other as they exit. CORINNE and PENELOPE attempt to sneak out.

>   GOODMAN
>   (continuing)
>   Stay right where you are.

They pout and murmur.

SNITCH stands by front door, blocks exit. Snitch pushed hard from behind, thrown inward as MARGARET enters front door.

She points COLT 45 between his eyes.

>   MARGARET
>   Sit down!

Snitch sits at a booth. Goodman's bewildered.

>   GOODMAN
>   How many more tricks up your
>   sleeve?

>   MARGARET
>   It's me you want. Let Jennifer
>   and the others go.

>   GOODMAN
>   I'm walking right out of here and
>   this beauty queen's coming with me.

Goodman slowly retracts to back door with Jennifer.

SAMUEL enters back door, stands behind Goodman. Corinne and Samuel's eyes meet. Samuel places toilet plunger handle to back of Goodman's head.

Snitch can't see the plunger, he sits in a booth eye-to-eye with tank gun muzzles.

The GRANNY holds a leash tightly on Samuel in b.g.

>   SAMUEL
>   Not so fast, Mr. Goodman. Put the
>   gun down and release the girl.

Goodman freezes. Margaret points her gun at Goodman.

                    GOODMAN
          Is that you, Sam?

                    SAMUEL
          It is I. And this ain't no toilet
          plunger.

                    GOODMAN
          Go ahead and shoot, Sam. The
          princess dies. You think about
          that.

Goodman continues to back up to rear door, holds pistol to
Jennifer's temple. He stands by her side.

Samuel holds plunger handle to Goodman's head, backs up too.
Bulldog growls.

Samuel sees Sarah smile. She dips sponge inside bottle of
sulfuric acid. Samuel frowns.

Snitch leaps from his seat, aims two guns to Margaret's head.
Margaret tosses her gun to floor. Goodman laughs.

AFTER A TENSE MOMENT OF SILENCE

Fluffy leaps into Goodman's face, claws extended OUCH!
Impact deflects gun BANG! Muzzle blast misses Jennifer by
millimeters.

Bulldog leaps, clamps onto Samuel's butt OW! OW!

Margaret knocks both guns out of Snitch's hands to the floor.

Samuel jams rubber end of toilet plunger onto Goodman's hand
against wall SQUISH!

The grannies grab Snitch and hold him.

                    SAMUEL
          I kept my bargain.

Bulldog lets go of Samuel.

Margaret doesn't bother to pick up the guns on floor.

Margaret, unarmed, slowly approaches Goodman.

Goodman, with a back heel kick, hits Samuel you know where.
Samuel crumples to his knees. Bulldog snarls inches from his
nose.

Sponge dabs his butt. Steaming vapors rise OUCH!

                    SAMUEL
                  (continuing)
        I repent. I repent.

Goodman points his 9mm right at Margaret's chest. Goodman's
ultra stressed, face red, lips quiver.

                    MARGARET
                  (calmly)
        Give it up, Goodman.

Goodman's eyes look wild. He breathes heavy, snorts like a
bull.

                    GOODMAN
                  (to Margaret)
        I've nothing to lose now. I'll do
        time, but you. You'll be in the
        grave where you belong!

He cocks the hammer CLICK! Squeezes trigger, fires point
blank range into Margaret's chest BLAM!

She's blown back three feet and falls down. Slowly, she gets
up.

One bar of the THEME SONG from the Terminator movie o.s.

                    SNITCH
        She's got a vest, shoot for the
        head.

Goodman aims. Muzzle flash parts Margaret's hair. She just
stands there, compassion in her eyes.

                    MARGARET
        Blanks! They're just blanks!

Goodman's totally shocked. He fires until the gun clicks
empty. Margaret calmly reaches for the gun.

Goodman cooperates, then he swings the gun to hit her in the
head.

Like a karate expert, Margaret blocks, hits Goodman with a
jabbing elbow thrust, then a swinging heel kick to the jaw.
He's down and out.

All the grannies and Jennifer cheer with victory. Fluffy
meows. Bulldog growls, tears Samuel's pants.

                    SARAH
                  (to Samuel)
        That'll be a lesson to defy the
        will of your elders.

                          SAMUEL
              Ouch! Get that beast off me.

Everyone in room laughs.

                          SARAH
              I want an oath. Swear it.

                          SAMUEL
              I will forevermore serve, protect,
              cherish and defend all
              grandmothers forever and ever,
              amen.

Bulldog stops biting.

                          SARAH
              I don't trust you.

EXT. STREET - DAY

GI GRANNIES dangle from snagged parachutes. They eat Granny
Apples. FBI CAR arrives. MARGARET hands over the stolen
money. FBI AGENT counts it.

                          MARGARET
              You don't trust grannies?

Granny Apple SPLATS ground by agent's feet. He puts money in
pocket. GRANNIES deliver SNITCH and GOODMAN. FBI AGENTS
handcuff, push them into back seat of car.

MARGARET approaches them. She's not angry or dominating in
any way. She's just a grandmother like any other grandmother.

                          SNITCH
              How did you do that? Slip blanks
              in our guns?

                          MARGARET
              Grannies are everywhere. You don't
              see us because you don't want to,
              but we're always with you. In
              restaurants, supermarkets, the
              beach, at work, and yes. In your
              homes!
                      (beat)
              Crime doesn't pay Mr. Goodman. You
              should have listened to my
              grandmother.

                          GOODMAN
                      (baffled)
              Your grandmother?

                         MARGARET
               Mizrabella!

Goodman's chin drops. FBI drive off. Goodman holds his
head. Snitch gently pats his head to comfort him.

INT. MARGARET'S HOUSE / LIVING ROOM - EVENING

All GRANNY ALLIES present watch the TV news. Corinne,
Samuel, Sarah not in attendance.

Teenage MAID serves bottles of "Happy Bowels Fiber Cocktail"
drinks.

                         MARGARET
                     (to Lanky)
               You can stay with us if you like.

                         LANKY
               I'm afraid of the American way of
               life.

Everyone laughs. Margaret points to the TV.

ON TV / NEWS SHOTS / PRISON LOCATIONS - EVENING

- - SNITCH pulls ping-pong balls from cage.

                         SNITCH
               I-eighteen. B-nine.

BIG DADDY, MAD DOG, and SPIKE sit at tables with CONVICTS.
Big Daddy raises his hand.

                         BIG DADDY
               Bingo!

Hard-core CONS flash cold icy stares.

- - GOODMAN plunges a cell toilet with a big mean PRISON
GUARD.

                         PRISON GUARD (V.O.)
                     (deep voice)
               Hurry up, Goodman. We have sixty-
               seven more to go.

GUARD looks straight at us, winks. She's a GRANNY!

ON TV / EXT. CITY HALL - DAY

- - CORINNE, the new POLICE CHIEF, stands by SAMUEL's side,
our new MAYOR. He speaks to GRANNIES on front steps of City
Hall.

SARAH stands behind Samuel with leash to his belt. BULLDOG growls. She jabs him with elbow.

                    SAMUEL (V.O.)
          This is your city. I work for you!

- - FRANK, sits in wheelchair oblivious to the world, mouth hangs limp.

JEANETTE and SUSAN stand beside him, use index fingers to make Frank smile for the TV camera. They both wear diamond engagement rings.

INT. BACK TO LIVING ROOM SCENE - EVENING

Phone RINGS. MARGARET answers it. Everyone's curious.

                    MARGARET
                 (on phone)
          Hello. What? You must be out of
          your mind. No, sir. I mean no
          disrespect.

Margaret stands to attention. LANKY points to TV.

                    LANKY
          Look!

Attention shifts from Margaret to TV.

ON TV - EXT. CITY HALL - DAY

FRANK's mouth wide open frozen in time.

Ticker tape caption runs along bottom of screen, "Read my mind. No more taxes."

CROWD of grannies CHEER. SARAH pinches SAMUEL'S ear. BULLDOG nips pant leg. He claps hands, smiles. She steps on his foot.

                    SAMUEL
          There will be commodes on every
          street corner in Lost Angus.
          Sparkling clean toilets for
          everyone!

CORINNE raises a sign, "Love Your Granny!" The VULTURE leaps into her arms. She lovingly kisses it.

CROWD cheers, toss hats and handbags into the air. They don't fall. Items stuck in tree branches.

INT. BACK TO LIVING ROOM SCENE - EVENING

Everyone stands and cheers, hug each other. MARGARET waves
her hands, sits down, still on phone.

                    MARGARET
               (on phone)
          We had no control over that.
          What? Don't be ridiculous. I
          apologize.

LANKY and BERTHA slow dance. They face MIZRABELLA. She
holds the crystal ball.

Bertha strips her clothes, reveals a wedding gown.

                    MIZRABELLA
          I pronounce you man and wife.

LANKY and BERTHA kiss. Everyone toasts the event.

                    MARGARET
          Shhh. Shush-up.

All fall silent.

INT. WHITE HOUSE / OVAL OFFICE - EVENING

A GRANNY (75) behind the President's desk, speaks into a red
phone. She sits back, feet crisscrossed on desk, smokes a
cigar.

Next to the President's name plate a placard reads, "Blame
Congress Not Me."

She places her own in front of it, "Don't argue, granny
knows best!" Then another beside it, "MEBOM and proud." And
one more, "Don't turn my crank!"

The two GRANNIES we saw at training camp in civilian clothes
stand silent. Stiff-jawed expressions, dressed in black with
dark sunglasses.

                    PRESIDENT'S GRANNY
               (defensively, on
                phone)
          He's gone to Arabia or someplace.
          He won't be back for another two
          weeks.
               (beat)
          I'll call the girls in Boston,
          that is, if you feel --

BACK TO SCENE

                    MARGARET
                  (on phone)
          Too old? You get me the stuff you
          bag of misery!

Margaret hangs up, smiles, raises glass high in air.

FLUFFY leaps to Margaret's lap, curls into a ball, purrs
contentedly.

Margaret looks right at us.

                    MARGARET
                  (continuing)
          Let's go to Washington!

                                        FADE OUT:

          The end.

AS CREDITS ROLL

EXT. HOLLYWOOD BOULEVARD - NIGHT

Disco / Rock-fusion MUSIC score.

- - ELDERLY people stroll sidewalks at night, window shop.
Dressed in colorful high-fashion clothes. SARAH strolls by
with her BULLDOG.

- - Granny COPS shove a TEENAGER in a patty wagon.
JENNIFER'S inside, she rattles steel window bars. FLUFFY
hisses.

DOWN THE STREET

- - TWO MEN (80) in convertible hotrod, top down, pull to
curb. LOLITA and DONNA exchange looks, shrug shoulders,
smile. They step in and away they go.

Their hair blows in the wind.

- - OLD MEN (90) dressed in biker gang colors, "Hollywood
Angels" stand by beautiful Harley Davidson choppers, eat hot
dogs, drink coffee, smoke pipes. They whistle to,

CORINNE, DEBBIE, PENELOPE. dressed like teenagers, blue
jeans/halter tops. MARGARET in skirt. They accept
invitation from the bikers, hop on the Harley's and take off.

- - COP CAR passes by. Cops are GRANNIES. Emblem on door
panel. A fist holding a lightening bolt, "MEBOM task force.
To serve and protect Lost Angus."

- - MARGARET sits on gas tank, hugs the old BIKER.   Her leg
extended. She waves to her elderly friends on sidewalk.

- - All the ALLY GRANNIES wave back.

INSERT

"The streets are safe once again. At least for the grannies!"

THE 7 DAY PLAN TO BE A BETTER CHRISTIAN!

SUNDAY -- This is a day of rest (see Saturday) of which no work is to be performed. Take full advantage of it! However, extend extra kindness to others. Read the Word, listen to Christian radio and watch TV for faith comes by "hearing" the Word of God.

MONDAY -- Drive your vehicle with patience towards others. Be changed at work. No more gossip, complaining, bad jokes. Just start being nice -- Biblically correct! Be cooperative. Can you do this for just one day?

TUESDAY -- Forget Me! Do a good thing for another. Open doors, buy someone a meal or gift, feed a stranger's parking meter. Give so you will receive. Give something! The Lord gives, so should you.

WEDNESDAY -- Compliment Day! Say something nice to someone, including one who may not like you. Be sincere about it! If someone needs help, go to their aid. Make someone smile today!

THURSDAY -- Distribute a Bible track. No tracks? Make or buy some! It is time you begin your ministry to the Lord to share the Good News. There are many hurting people who need the Lord and it is your responsibility to introduce them to Him. Using tracks make the job easy!

FRIDAY -- Day of forgiveness! When you forgive others transgressions, you are released from the anguish within yourself. It is easy to do! Start the process today! See Tuesday and Wednesday's instructions. Life is so much easier to live and great mercy and blessing arrive when you forgive!

SATURDAY -- Rest if this is the Sabbath you honor or donate; time, items, food, or money to the homeless shelters. Do not forget the poor! Visit or call a relative or friend. Express your appreciation for what the Lord has given you! Share with others what you have and the Lord will give you even more!

Free Bible Tracks For SASE!   **EACH DAY**   Contact Us For Bible Tracks!

START the day right by greeting the Lord and giving thanks for all He has done and what He will do for you in the future. **END** the day right by expressing your gratitude to the Lord.

SPEAK often to the Lord, as he is your best friend. Remember, he wants to handle every detail in your life, even the small stuff. Do not become so busy in your day you leave Him out of your life.

WHEN you pray just speak as you would to a friend. There is no need for theatrical displays of emotions or insincerity. If you fall short, do not turn your face away from the Lord and hide. Take the issue to Him.

WHAT will you give to the Lord if He grants your request? Will you simply say thank you and forget Him until you need something else later? The Lord sees the suffering of the sick and poor. Why not pledge to help them? Make your promise and keep it! Do it now before you recieve. This is faith in action.

SPREAD the Word of God. You may not be a minister, but you can distribute tracks. Leave them everywhereyou go. Keep some on your person each day. Your reward shall be great! Write us for tracts!

TITHE to the Lord. Give and you shall recieve more! Give to churches, ministries, homeless shelters, or where there is dire need. A perfect expression of love for others! God's System Never Fails!

PRINT AND DISTRIBUTE TO OTHERS!

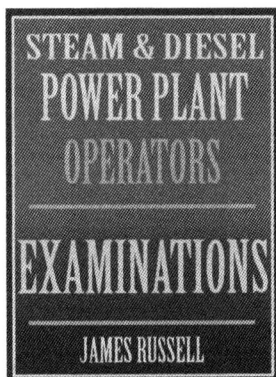

www.ingramcontent.com/pod-product-compliance
Lightning Source LLC
Chambersburg PA
CBHW081153090426
42736CB00017B/3302